295
11

WHAT IS A SAINT?

IS VOLUME

46

OF THE

Twentieth Century Encyclopedia of Catholicism

UNDER SECTION

IV

*THE MEANS OF REDEMPTION*

IT IS ALSO THE

3RD

VOLUME IN ORDER OF PUBLICATION

*Edited by* **HENRI DANIEL-ROPS** *of the Académie Française*

# WHAT IS A SAINT?

### By *JACQUES DOUILLET*

*Translated from the French by DONALD ATTWATER*

HAWTHORN BOOKS · PUBLISHERS · *New York*

*First Edition,* October, 1958

NIHIL OBSTAT

Carolus Davis, S.T.L.

*Censor Deputatus*

IMPRIMATUR

✠ Georgius L. Craven

*Episcopus Sebastopolis, Vicarius Generalis*
Westmonasterii, die XXVIII MAII MCMLVIII

# CONTENTS

# PART ONE

# HOLINESS

# CHAPTER I

# THE HOLY PEOPLE

For our purpose, the answer to the question "What is a saint?" has special interest and outstanding importance when it is given by the earliest Christian writer. There can be no evidence more authentic than that which is drawn from the sources, especially, of course, when the writer is one inspired by the Holy Spirit.

The oldest writings in Christian literature are St Paul's letters. Taking one of these letters at random, that which he wrote to his friends at Philippi in Macedonia, we find that it begins: "Paul and Timothy, the servants of Jesus Christ, to all the *saints* in Christ Jesus that are at Philippi, with their pastors and deacons; Grace and peace be yours from God who is our Father, and from the Lord Jesus Christ." And it ends: "Greet all the *saints* in Christ Jesus. The brethren who are with me send you their greeting; greeting, too, from all the *saints*, especially those who belong to the emperor's household. The grace of our Lord Jesus Christ be with your spirit. Amen." Other communities are addressed in similar terms: ". . . to the church of God at Corinth, to those who have been *sanctified* in Christ Jesus, and called to be *holy* . . ."; ". . . to the church of God which is at Corinth and to all the *saints* in the whole of Achaia . . ."; ". . . to the *saints* at Colossae, our brethren who believe in Jesus Christ"; ". . . to all those at Rome whom God loves and has called to be *holy*, grace and peace from God our Father, and from the Lord Jesus Christ."

Evidently for Paul the saints are all the faithful, all those

newly converted people who made up the first Christian communities, whom he does not hesitate to address in pretty un-
flattering terms: "You must deaden, then, those passions in
you which belong to earth, fornication and impurity, lust and
evil desire, and that love of money which is an idolatry. These
are what bring down God's vengeance on the unbelievers, and
such was your own behaviour, too, while you lived among them.
Now it is your turn to have done with it all, resentment, anger,
spite, insults, foul-mouthed utterance . . ." (Col. 3. 5–8); "Make
no mistake about it; it is not the debauched, the idolaters, the
adulterous, it is not the effeminate, the sinners against nature,
the dishonest, the misers, the drunkards, the bitter of speech,
the extortioners that will inherit the kingdom of God. That
is what some of you once were; but now you have been washed
clean, now you have been *sanctified* . . ." (1 Cor. 6. 9–11).

What curious words! We do not generally think of saints as
people like that. What is this sanctification that has suddenly
transformed debauchees and idolaters, thieves and drunkards?

To find out what St Paul was driving at when he called the
members of his communities "saints", we have to turn to the
earlier books of the Bible and examine the idea of holiness in
the Old Testament. Paul was, as he himself emphasized, a Jew
of the Jews; he was brought up on their sacred books, and, even
after the proclamation of the Gospel, they remained God's word
for him, its integrity undiminished. And Christ's followers, to
whom he talked and wrote, were spiritually children of
Abraham, even those of them who had come from paganism.

## HOLINESS BEFORE CHRIST

### "Holy" as opposed to "profane"[1]

In the third verse of the second chapter of Genesis, the first
book of the Bible, there is a short phrase that perfectly ex-

---

[1] Nowadays the word *profane* generally has a depreciatory flavour in
English. But its primary meaning does not bear this; it simply means
"not sacred": Latin *profanus*, in front of (i.e., outside) the temple. In
Latin, "holiness" is *sanctitas*, the adjective "holy" is *sanctus*, and the
noun "saint" is also *sanctus*. [*Trans.*]

presses one of the constituent elements of holiness. After the seven days of creation, the sacred writer says that "God gave the seventh day his blessing, and *hallowed* it" (Gen. 2. 3). He means by this that in every week there shall be six profane, or "secular", days and one sacred day. During the six days men shall work at will for business or pleasure, but there shall be another day that God has sanctified, a holy day, that is, one consecrated by God and to God. This will be God's special part in the week. Both in Hebrew and in Greek the words used suggest a separation, a setting apart, something reserved for God.

In the very next book, Exodus (3. 5), we read that when Moses drew near to the burning bush, God said to him: "Do not come nearer; rather take the shoes from thy feet, thou art standing on *holy* ground." Here we have the same distinction between profane and sacred. God gave man the whole earth, and the soles of his shoes can beat out paths wherever he wills; but there are certain privileged spots that are reserved to God because he has shown forth his presence there. These are *holy places*, and man must tread them only with feet bare.

Later on, when a temple had been built at Jerusalem as the dwelling-place of Jehovah, people could walk freely on the terraces and in the forecourt; but there was an inner sanctuary, the *Holy of holies* into which only the priests were allowed to enter, for there they came into direct relation with God. The city in which this temple was built was called the *Holy City*, and the priests who served the temple were themselves called holy, since they were set apart from other men ("seculars") and consecrated wholly to Jehovah's service.

Every profanation of holy ground or a sanctified thing was at once visited with God's punishment as a human trespass on the divine domain. Here is a passage which, among several like it, bears striking testimony to the Israelites' fear of touching whatever was hallowed by God's presence. When David resolved to bring back the Ark of the Covenant from Kirjath-jearim to Jerusalem, they put it "on a newly-made waggon, with Abinadab's sons, Oza and Ahio, for its drivers. He it was who had had charge of it . . . but now they took it away from his house, with Ahio walking before it, while David and the Israelites played music. . . . They had reached the threshing-floor of Nachon, when the oxen began to kick and tilted the ark to one side; whereupon Oza put out his hand and caught hold of it. Rash deed of his, that provoked the divine anger; the Lord smote him, and he died there beside the ark" (2 Kings 6. 3–7).

We have the benefit of divine teaching that has been given since those days, and we know that there was no moral fault in Oza's spontaneous action; he meant well, and God could not hold it against him. But David was so impressed by the fatal accident that he left the Ark in a nearby house; it was not till three months later, when he learned that the presence of the Ark had brought blessing on the household, that its removal to Jerusalem was finally carried through. This respect mingled with fear that filled profane persons with awe when they had to approach things that God had sanctified reminds us some-times of the superstitious fears of primitive peoples; and we may wonder whether there be not an altogether genuine and admirable sense of God's holiness behind such rudimentary forms.

### "Holy, holy, holy, Lord . . ."

Holy places are forbidden ground to the profane, mere con-tact with sanctified things is so awesome, because they share in God's own holiness, which is the source and reason of all holiness.

God's holiness. What is it? When Christians sing "Holy, holy, holy is the Lord God of hosts" at Mass, they think today in the first place of God's supreme perfection. They declare that all the virtues and good qualities they admire in holy people are found in God in infinite measure and perfection, without fault or blemish. Holiness is in that case synonymous with moral perfection.

This interpretation is not wrong. But when, twenty-seven centuries ago, the prophet Isaias heard seraphim in the Temple crying out to one another "Holy, holy, holy is the Lord God of hosts", when the bronze doors shook and the place was filled with smoke, the awe that filled him shows that this is not the first sense that he gave to the word "holy". To his prophetical mind it meant above all a mysterious, awe-inspiring power, a sovereign majesty in whose presence man is no more than dust and ashes (Gen. 18. 27).

Things are holy because they are set apart from the profane world; just so, God is holy because he is not part of the world. The world is not separate from him, because the world exists only through him; but he is not a being among other beings. He surpasses them infinitely, and compared with his their existence is only a nothingness, for it depends entirely on his almighty will.

When we talk about God, our poor human words have to find analogies, similarities, between his creatures and him: we have to speak of his power or his justice or his goodness as if there were a common measure between the power or justice of an earthly ruler and divine power or justice, between the goodness of an earthly father and the goodness of our Father in Heaven. But there is no such common measure. God is not in the series of beings that we know or can imagine, not even if we try to think of him as the infinitely great apex of the series. He controls and rules the series and, as the philosophers say, transcends it.

By a stupendous intuition, by a revelation, the prophets of Israel "felt" what theologians have tried for centuries to formulate for us, what mystics, such as St John of the Cross, have occasionally succeeded in faintly suggesting to us.

It is impossible to put God's holiness into words, because our language is designed to deal with the people and things that we live amongst; and it is precisely the characteristic of God's holiness that there is no possible comparison between created beings and God who created them. But the prophets suggested what that holiness is by their attitude before the God whom no man can see and remain alive (Exod. 33. 20): their reverent fear, their awe at his coming, are not the result of superstitious terror, but the proper reaction of one who is conscious that he has been created out of nothing.

Perhaps at some time in our life we have experienced a veritable religious emotion under the influence of solitude and silence, on a mountain at night, for instance, or on the sea or during a long desert journey, and have known the presence of him who created mountain, sea and desert at the same time as he created us: lost in that immensity we felt an awe not unlike that of the prophets when confronted by God's holiness, and we were able to understand their language.

God is awe-inspiring, but he is not cruel; rather does he radiate goodness, and those who tremble before his majesty are at the same time drawn to him. God is apart from the world, but he is not absent from it; the earth is his kingdom. God is full of unutterable mystery, but he makes himself known; he has revealed himself.

*The Holy People*

God chose the Hebrew people for this revelation. He willed to sanctify this people. This means that it had to be set apart from other peoples for the special destiny that he intended for it.

The whole Old Testament recognizes the immensity of this privilege, and proudly it proclaims it. True it is that Jehovah's rule would one day have to be extended to all the peoples of the world, but it was for Israel to spread that rule. There was a covenant, an alliance, between Jehovah and his people. In the nineteenth chapter of the book of Exodus we read that, in the third month after leaving Egypt, Israel camped in the wilderness before Mount Sinai. Moses went up the mountain, "to meet God", and Jehovah said to him: "A message to the race of Jacob; to Israel's sons proclaim it: You have seen for yourselves what I did to the Egyptians, how I carried you as if on eagle's wings, and took you up into my care. Listen, then, to my voice, and keep your covenant with me; and I, to whom all the earth belongs, will single you out among its peoples to be my own. You shall serve me as a royal priesthood, as a consecrated nation."

Those few pregnant words sum up what it was that made God's people a holy people: after the affirmation of Jehovah's rule over the whole earth, they record a choice and a consecration like to the choice and consecration of priests among the people. The people did not choose its mission, any more than the priests consecrated themselves. They were men of God because it was God who commissioned them. He gave them liturgical and sacrificial duties; in the midst of the profane, they were witnesses to the Unseeable and Unutterable. They were sanctified by him, and they were to sanctify their brethren. Through them the thrice-holy God raised his chosen people to himself.

But the people itself was to have a mission to the world resembling that of the priests in their midst. It, a nation of priests, had in its turn to witness to the Unseeable and Unutterable among the profane peoples; sanctified by him, they were to sanctify others. And the whole history of Israel—even the history of her wars, whose victories and defeats were seen as divine sanctions—is simply a setting forth of God's holiness made manifest in his people, manifested gloriously or sorrowfully according to whether his people was faithful or faithless to its mission. For Jehovah's promise given through Moses was conditional: if you "keep your covenant with me".

*Holiness through the Law*

That the Hebrew people had been chosen by God for his own meant that it had special obligations towards him: the holy people was not free to live like the peoples that were still profane. That which is holy belongs to God: holy men and women must wholly obey the will of him who possesses them, for that is the only way in which they can acknowledge that they are his. God's will in respect of his people was set out in the Law, and the holy people had to sanctify itself by observing Jehovah's law exactly.

The Law included many ritual regulations: their number, and the importance that the sacred writer attached to them, is very surprising to us. For example, the third book of the Bible, Leviticus, enumerates at length the animals that were to be looked on as "impure". Whatever may have been the origin of this distinction between pure and impure things, even if that origin must be looked for in religions that preceded that of Jehovah, it is certain that at the time when the laws of Leviticus were drawn up the legislator's object was to compel the holy people to treat the all-holy God with respect, and at the same time to respect themselves. "All that creeps along the ground must be held in abomination, and never used for food. . . . Keep your persons undefiled, touching no such thing, for fear of contamination. I am the Lord your God; you must be set apart, the servants of a God who is set apart. Do not contaminate yourselves with any of these beasts that creep along the ground. I am the Lord your God, who rescued you from the land of Egypt; I am set apart and you must be set apart like me" (Lev. 11. 41–6).

What we see there is simply a ritual purity, whose observance is no doubt a homage to God because of the reverent submission to which it testifies; but as yet it is evidence of only an elementary form of religion. Later on we find that the great aim of the prophets is morally to educate the holy people, so that they may gradually go on from outward purity to inward purity, from ritual holiness to spiritual holiness, till the day comes when they understand that sin is, not the material disregard of a prohibition, but a man's rebellion when he refuses to reflect God's righteousness and goodness in his own soul.

Who is it, Lord, that will make his home in thy tabernacle,
rest on the mountain where thy sanctuary is?
One that guides his steps without fault, and gives to all their
due;

one whose heart is all honest purpose, who utters no treacherous
  word,
never defrauds a friend, or slanders a neighbour.
He scorns the reprobate, keeping his reverence for such as fear
  God,
and is true, come what may, to his pledged word;
lends without usury, and takes no bribe to condemn the
  innocent.
He who so lives will stand firm for ever. (Ps. 14)

That is the picture of the just, the holy man, a faithful
keeper of the Covenant.

And so for several centuries the children of Israel tried, by
being righteous, to correspond with their calling as members of
the holy people.

## The Law could not make Saints

When St Paul wrote to his communities in the terms that
have been quoted at the beginning of this chapter, he had
already been aware for some years that, although it had been
prescribed by God, the Law was powerless to make saints.

As a young man he had, like so many of his ancestors among
the Israelites, longed for perfection, and he hoped, as they
hoped, to attain, through scrupulously exact observance of the
Law, a state of holiness that would be a reflection of Jehovah's
holiness. But after what happened on the road to and in
Damascus, he knew that he had laboured in vain: that no man,
be he Jew or Gentile, can avoid sin by his own efforts. That is
what he taught to the saints of the church at Rome—and how
forcibly! But sin is incompatible with holiness: for the sinner
tries to keep for himself something that belongs to God, and
his movement towards God is countered by a power that draws
him away from God.

Moreover, it was not only transgression of the Law that stood
in the way of holiness: a minute observance of it could do so
too, for it focused a man's attention on himself and tended

to make him forget his creaturely state. He could think of himself as a just man, who had given to God all that God had the right to expect from him. He could as it were stand up and justify himself before God, as if he were confronting an examiner who was powerful and severe, but still human. That was the state of mind of the Pharisee in the parable. The fact of being a sinner is an offence against God's holiness; the consciousness of being irreproachably righteous is no less an offence.

At the time when the Messiah was expected, those who had heard the call to holiness were seeking to follow a dangerous passage between the rocks of sin on one side and of pharisaism on the other. Doubtless there were many who succeeded—but not thanks to their own efforts. By anticipation, and without knowing it, they already shared in the holiness of him whom their prophets had foretold and for whom they were looking.

## CHRISTIAN HOLINESS

### You alone, Jesus Christ, are the Holy One

It is tempting to think that holiness for man is a dream, a wonderful idea but quite unpractical. For something to be destined for God, to be handed back in its wholeness to him who gave it being, is perhaps possible when it is a matter of a thing to be used in religious worship: any profane use of it can be forbidden. But when it is a human being? In that case an external setting-apart is not enough. While keeping his own personality, a man has to be able to direct his activities and the very roots of his being towards God, to such a degree that not the slightest trace of selfishness or earthly enthralment is left in him. When we have caught some faint glimpse of what God's holiness is, we ask ourselves how man could ever suppose that he would one day be able to act on God's call to be holy as he is holy—man who is so weak, burdened with an inheritance of depravity, his inclinations and instincts corrupted by original sin.

It needed the incarnation of the Word, it needed Christ, God made man, to make this ideal of holiness possible and actual. Human nature was at last sanctified in Jesus, for he is truly man, like us even in all our weaknesses, save .sin; yet that human soul and body of his are wholly God's, are wholly turned to God. From the first moment of his earthly existence on the day of the Annunciation, till his last breath on Golgotha when he gave back his soul to his Father, there was not an instant that was withdrawn from self-sacrifice: "Father, may your will be done, not mine."

Christ's whole life belonged to God because it was wholly inspired by God; or, more exactly, it belonged to the Father because it had been offered up by the Son. The mystery of Christ's holiness is bound up with the mystery of the Blessed Trinity. In that eternal Trinity the Son reflects the whole splendour of the Father, because the Father holds back nothing and gives all to the Son. But neither does the Son hold back anything, he gives himself wholly to the Father by love.

When the Son willed to become incarnate, to take a human soul and body, he transposed that will of total self-offering into the human key. The holiness of the Son of man is purely and simply the enfleshing of the holiness of the uncreated Word. That is why Christ is called in the New Testament, not only "holy", but The Holy One. It is a proper name, attributed to him personally (Apoc. 3. 7), just as Isaias said of God, before it had been learned to distinguish three persons in him, "His name is Holy".

It is with all this in mind that the Church puts into our mouths at Mass, on the days when the *Gloria in excelsis* is said, the words written above: "You alone are the Holy One, you alone are Lord, you alone, Jesus Christ, are the Most High...."

## In Christ Jesus

The divine Word did not will to sanctify human nature and remain secluded in this unique holiness, but to enable his human brethren to share in it. They too were to be able to become holy, "in Christ Jesus".

That expression, "in Christ Jesus", was always on St Paul's pen, understandably enough, for this mystery of incorporation into Christ is at the heart of all Christian life. The sins of the former sinner are forgiven when man the sinner, the "old man", dies at the moment that he becomes a member of Christ by baptism. By baptism Christ has made him have part in his own death, in order that man when he comes up out of the baptismal water may also have part in his resurrection. He stands then before the thrice-holy God as a new man, for it is no longer he who lives, but Christ is living in him.

> In our baptism, we have been buried with him, died like him, that so, just as Christ was raised up by his Father's power from the dead, we too might live and move in a new kind of existence. We have to be closely fitted into the pattern of his resurrection, as we have been into the pattern of his death; we have to be sure of this, that our former nature [the "old man"] has been crucified with him, and the living power of our guilt annihilated, so that we are the slaves of guilt no longer. Guilt makes no more claim on a man who is dead. And if we have died with Christ, we have faith to believe that we shall share his life. We know that Christ, now he has risen from the dead, cannot die any more; death has no more power over him; the death he died was a death, once for all, to sin; the life he now lives is a life that looks towards God. And you, too, must think of yourselves as dead to sin, and alive with a life that looks towards God, through Jesus our Lord. (Rom. 6. 4–11.)

Thus the first impediment to human holiness is swept away: the burden of sin. And the second likewise, trust in one's own efforts and the pharisaical self-satisfaction that goes with it; for the Christian knows that his new-found spiritual integrity is not due to his own goodness but to him who gave his life to save him. It is his ambition to keep this integrity, and to go forward in it day by day; he trusts that he will never again depart from God's will, but rather become more perfect in fulfilling it:

but this will not be by looking to himself for the ability to do so. For henceforth he who alone was perfect on this earth is living in him.

## A New Life

Obviously the effects of baptism do not come about like a sort of magical operation which will transform the baptized person without there being any deep-seated psychological change in him. If he is to be truly incorporated in Christ and partake of his holiness, he must for the future live like Christ, be animated by his Spirit.

But there are underlying evil forces always at work, with which he who is sanctified is continually in conflict: they are what St Paul calls "the flesh" or "nature", not only bodily passions but the soul's disorderly tendencies too. But by God's mercy this struggle is no longer what it used to be, a wearisome endeavour to conform to a burdensome law.

> Let me say this: learn to live and move in the spirit; then there is no danger of your giving way to the impulses of corrupt nature. . . . It is by letting the spirit lead you that you free yourselves from the yoke of the law. It is easy to see what effects proceed from corrupt nature; they are such things as adultery, impurity, incontinence, luxury, idolatry, witchcraft, feuds, quarrels, jealousies, outbursts of anger, rivalries, dissensions, factions, spite, murder, drunkenness and debauchery. I warn you, as I have warned you before, that those who live in such a way will not inherit God's kingdom. Whereas the spirit yields a harvest of love, joy, peace, patience, kindness, generosity, forbearance, gentleness, faith, courtesy, temperateness, purity. No law can touch lives such as these; those who belong to Christ have crucified nature, with all its passions, all its impulses. Since we live by the spirit, let the spirit be our rule of life. . . . (Gal. 5. 16–25.)

The Spirit, that is, that has brought those who are Christ's to that state of integrity without which there is no holiness, the Spirit that enables them to fight perseveringly to keep that integrity. They refuse to give in to temptations that used to over-

come them, not out of obedience to God's commands alone,
but because they are conscious that Christ is present within
them and they cannot bear to sully that presence.

> Now you have been washed clean, now you have been sancti-
> fied, now you have been justified in the name of the Lord Jesus,
> by the Spirit of the God we serve.... Have you never been told
> that your bodies belong to the body of Christ? And am I to
> take what belongs to Christ and make it one with a harlot?
> God forbid.... Surely you know that your bodies are the shrines
> of the Holy Spirit, who dwells in you. And he is God's gift to
> you, so that you are no longer your own masters. A great price
> was paid to ransom you; glorify God by making your bodies
> the shrines of his presence. (I Cor. 6. 11–20.)

There is no holiness without mastery of the body. There is
no holiness if the way of the Cross be avoided. That cross is not
there simply once, on the day of baptism; it is always there, a
fixture, so that the faithful man or woman, the *fidelis*, goes on
crucifying nature with all its passions and impulses. The saint
has to mortify himself: the Holy Spirit requires this of him—
it is evidence of love.

## A Life of Love

A pure, sinless, mortified life is the negative aspect of holiness, and a very impressive aspect, for such integrity can be
maintained only at the cost of numberless positive efforts made
under the pressure of a real love for God. But there are other
aspects of this new life. Ordinary things, those that are not
"crucifying", those even that are agreeable, have to be done in
a new spirit, a spirit of sonship, of thankfulness, and like a
hymn of praise: "In eating, in drinking, in all that you do, do
everything as for God's glory" (1 Cor. 10. 31).

The Christian cannot be like his Master and be led by his
spirit unless he is alight with charity and love. For Christ loved.
"But here, as if God meant to prove how well he loves us, it
was while we were still sinners that Christ, in his appointed
time, died for us", wrote St Paul to the Roman Christians, and

in St John's gospel (15. 13) our Lord underlines it: "This is the greatest love a man can show, that he should lay down his life for his friends." Holiness is to love as Jesus loved.

To love is to prefer, to choose this rather than that. It is to give up one's own preferences in favour of God's. It is to love the brethren as Jesus loves them: and he loves each one of them with a personal love, which did not stop short of sacrificing his life for them. The way is open for those who want to follow Christ; they are indwelt by the Holy Spirit and they know what he wants of them. The moral ideal of the holy man is expressed once for all at the beginning of the thirteenth chapter of the first Epistle to the Corinthians: "Charity is patient, is kind; charity feels no envy; charity is never perverse or proud, never insolent; does not claim its rights, cannot be provoked, does not brood over an injury; takes no pleasure in wrongdoing, but rejoices at the victory of truth; sustains, believes, hopes, endures, to the last" (1 Cor. 13. 4–7).

That is the way holy men or women will live until "the day of the Lord Jesus", when everlasting happiness will begin for them. In that day, everything that opposed God's reign in them will be finally done away with, and they will be confirmed in holiness for ever and ever.

## The New Holy People

Thus the holy people with whom Jehovah entered into a covenant, that it might be the witness and herald of his divine holiness amidst the other peoples, has given place to a new holy people; and this new people is not recruited by physical generation, but by the incorporation in Christ of all the baptized whatever their origin, whether Jewish or heathen. This new holy people is the Church, whose head is Christ and whose members are the faithful. And it is as true to say that the faithful are members of Christ as that the faithful are members of the Church.

It is through the Church that each of the faithful has been given baptism. It is she who breaks the Bread of fellowship to them. It is she who teaches them and governs them. None of them can persevere in holiness if he be separated from the others, for Christ has allotted missions as well as gifts among them. "Some he has appointed to be apostles, others to be prophets, others to be evangelists, or pastors, or teachers. They are to order the lives of the faithful, minister to their needs, build up the frame of Christ's body, until we all realize our common unity through faith in the Son of God, and fuller knowledge of him. So we shall reach perfect manhood, that maturity which is proportioned to the completed growth of Christ" (Eph. 4. 11–13).

So the personal sanctification of those who believe in Christ is brought about within the Christian community. The sanctification of those who do not yet believe in him has to be brought about by the Christian community. Formerly, the mission of the holy people, a "kingdom of priests", was to make the all-holy God known to the gentile peoples. Now, the Church of Christ, really sanctified by him, has even more the duty of being, amidst the peoples of mankind, the point of departure for the sanctification, the hallowing, of the world.

## The Members of the Holy People

It is unhappily true that many of those who had been numbered among the holy people because they had been called to sanctification, many of those whom St Paul greeted as members of the churches, violated the holiness which had been theirs. Paul's letters are poignant evidence of his ceaseless struggle to keep them in love for Jesus; but he does not conceal that some of them could have no part in Christ's kingdom.

But all the rest, all those who remain faithful, steady in faith, rooted in hope, persevering in charity, are to be considered as holy, "saints". Holiness is not an "honour" reserved to certain people: every Christian is called to holiness; it is the common lot of all the faithful. If they are really animated by Christ's spirit, as they ought to be, his spirit will not suffer them to be stopped short of their end, which is life in God. They will be saved. There are not three categories among those called to holiness: viz., those who refuse and are lost; those who accept wholeheartedly and are saints; and, between these extremes, those who are content to be saved without being saints. There is no distinction between "being saved" and "being a saint"; to be saved, one must be holy. It is in this sense that we declare in the Creed that we believe in the communion, that is, the fellowship, of the saints.

At the same time it is true that there are great differences of supernatural worth between the saints in this fellowship. There is nothing surprising about that: in the natural order, everyone has a rational understanding, but only a few are geniuses and there is an enormous mass of middling minds. There are analogous differences in the supernatural order: there are those who have received much from God and have responded generously to his goodness; and there are those who have been given only one talent, or who have not made the most of what they have received, much or little.

There are those among the holy people who realize what is called for by Christ's presence in them, and they give him love for love. Attracted by their example, others try to follow them, but succeed only in moving slowly. And then there are the laggards, the hesitant, the capricious, those who are afraid to give themselves yet do it all the same. All those, it may well be hoped, will be saved. And in principle it is right that they should be called saints, as St Paul does call them.

But actual usage now reserves the title of saint to those who march in front and give example to Christian people; to those whose lives give proof of unquestionable holiness, of whom the Church is ready to declare that they have attained Paradise and are now living in everlasting blessedness with Christ.

It is especially with reference to these that the question is asked, "What is a saint?"; and to them we will now turn. But it was necessary first of all to examine what there is in common between them and the other members of God's holy people, for their pre-eminent position does not cut them off from their fellow Christians. Between them and the general body there is no difference in kind but only one of degree: they exemplify in fine fashion what every Christian must want to be if he has grasped the meaning of his Christian vocation.

# CHAPTER II

# SOME EXAMPLES

In trying to give some idea of Christian holiness in the preceding pages we have relied principally on the teaching of St Paul. He put what he taught into practice, and did not fear to write "Follow my example, as I follow the example of Christ". Were we to examine the details of his life we should learn what a saint is, not theoretically, but in a concrete, living way. However, we prefer to widen our field of inquiry rather than stick to one example, however excellent.

Accordingly, we will take a few examples from the whole of the Church's history, chosen from among those saints who are known from authentic documents. They are very different one from another, both as persons and in the times at which they lived; we shall then be more easily able to see what they had in common, which is holiness. This is a short book, and in sketching their portraits we must be satisfied with a few broad lines; but we will do our best to select the most significant characteristics and not to give any false impression.

## ST IGNATIUS OF ANTIOCH

During a brief persecution at the beginning of the second century, probably in the year 107, a bishop of Antioch, named Ignatius, was arrested and condemned to death. It was at a time when the Roman circus needed a good supply of malefactors every month, to be thrown to wild beasts, and Ignatius was to be one of these victims.

He was taken to Rome in charge of a squad of ten soldiers,

and the first part of the journey was by sea to Macedonia. At the various ports of call the local Christian communities, informed in advance of his coming, came to greet him and to give him as much help as they could. From one of these delegations Ignatius learned that the faithful in Rome might try to get a mitigation of his sentence, and he at once sent a letter ahead to them. We still have the text of it, and it tells us that Ignatius, instead of welcoming the suggestion, implored his Roman brethren to give up any such idea.

> Only ask for me that I may be strong, within and without, so that I may be Christian in heart as well as in words, in deeds as well as in name. . . .
>
> I implore you to spare me untimely kindness. Let me be food for wild beasts, for thus shall I be able to reach God. I am God's wheat, to be ground by animals' teeth into Christ's good bread. . . . When the world cannot see even my body, then shall I be a true follower of Jesus Christ. Beseech him that I may become a sacrifice to God through the teeth of those savage creatures.
>
> Just now I am in chains, learning to desire nothing. From Syria to Rome, by land and sea, by day and night, I am even now fighting with wild beasts, chained as I am to ten leopards— I mean the soldiers who guard me: the more courteously they are treated the worse they get. Their brutality is a school that trains me every day—"but that is not where my justification lies". I am impatient for the beasts that await me, and I hope they will be hungry! If need be I will coax them to make short work of me and not hang back as they have done with some; if they do that, I will make them come on.
>
> Please do not interfere: I know what is good for me. I am at last beginning to be a real disciple. May nothing, seen or unseen, seduce me from happily attaining Jesus Christ! Come fire or cross, struggles with fierce beasts, breaking of bones and mangling of limbs, shattering of my whole body, come all the Devil's cruellest torments upon me, if only I may reach Christ Jesus![1]

[1] The whole letter is splendid. There is a translation of it in J. A. Kleist's *Epistles of St Clement of Rome and St Ignatius of Antioch* (London, 1950). The communion-verse in the Mass of the saint on February 1st is taken from the letter.

Ignatius was a man of sound sense, and he composedly gave sensible and thought-out advice to the faithful who came to meet him and to the Romans themselves. But he was one of those who love God, in Christ, and love him passionately; only God counted and death was gain, for death would establish him in God. He did not want death or torture: what he did want was he whom death would give him. "Let me copy my God's own passion," he wrote. "My earthly desires have been crucified,[1] and the fire of love for earthly things is quenched in me; only a 'living water' murmurs within, and it says 'Come to the Father'."

## ST PERPETUA AND ST FELICITY

About a century after the martyrdom of St Ignatius, in the year 203, five catechumens were arrested in Carthage. Among them were two women, a slave-girl named Felicity, who was with child, and Perpetua, a young wife, twenty-two years old with a baby at her breast.

They were baptized after the proceedings against them had been begun, and a few days later they were shut up in the common prison, herded in semi-darkness with other prisoners and at the mercy of the brutality of their guards. Two deacons were appointed to do what they could for them, and these bribed the jailers to allow the prisoners to go sometimes to a better part of the prison. There Perpetua could suckle her child, and after some days she obtained leave to keep him with her. "At once," she says, "I got better, being relieved of my trouble and anxiety about my baby." She wrote down a detailed account of the dreams or visions by which, during her imprisonment, she was strengthened and encouraged for the ordeal to come.

Perpetua's father, a pagan, at first tried to bully her into denying her faith; later he fell at her feet, kissing her hands

[1] Or possibly, "He whom I love has been crucified"; cf. *op. cit.*, pp. 83, 136. [*Trans.*]

and imploring her in the name of her family and his own grey
hairs not to bring sorrow upon them all by her resolution. "He
called me, not 'daughter', but 'lady'. And I grieved for his
misery . . . and comforted him, saying that what would happen
in court would be as God willed, and that we must trust in
his power, not our own."

At the trial her father was there with her baby, beseeching
her to have pity on the child and to sacrifice to the gods. So,
too, the judge: "Spare your father's old age and your son's
babyhood. Offer sacrifice for the welfare of the emperors."—
"I will not," she replied. "Are you a Christian?" she was asked,
and she answered that she was. Then the judge told her father
to stand aside, and someone hit him with a stick. "I sorrowed
for my father as though I had myself been struck," wrote
Perpetua, "and I grieved that his old age should be so unhappy.
Then sentence was passed on us all—we were condemned to
the wild beasts. As I had been suckling my baby in prison I at
once sent the deacon Pomponius to fetch the child from my
father; but he would not give him up."

Meanwhile, the slave-girl Felicity, who was in the eighth
month of pregnancy, was very disturbed: the games were at
hand, and her execution would be postponed, for by Roman
law a pregnant woman could not be put to death. She was unhappy at the thought of suffering later on with common
criminals and without the support of her fellow Christians; so
they all prayed together that they might not be separated, and
three days before the games her labour began. One of the
warders jeered at her: "You are groaning now," he said. "What
will you do when you are thrown to the beasts, which you did
not care about when you refused to sacrifice?" And Felicity
answered: "Now I myself suffer what I am suffering; but then
there will be Another in me who will suffer for me, because
I am to suffer for him." She gave birth to a girl, whom a woman
of the Christian community adopted.

On the day of their passion, all went gaily from the prison to
the amphitheatre. "Perpetua came last, with shining steps,

true bride of Christ and darling of God, her piercing gaze abashing all eyes. Felicity, too, rejoicing to come from blood to blood, from the midwife to the gladiator, to be washed after childbearing in a second baptism." At the gate officials tried to dress the men as priests of Saturn and the women as priestesses of Ceres, but they refused. "We have come here of our own free will," said Perpetua, "to make our freedom clear. We pledged our lives to do nothing of this sort. And you agreed." The commandant admitted this, and they went into the arena in their ordinary clothes, Perpetua singing aloud.

For the two women the keepers had a savage cow ready, a most unusual animal at the games, chosen in mockery of their sex. They were stripped and wrapped in nets; but the sight of them—one a gracious girl, the other fresh from childbirth with milk dripping from her breasts—so shocked the crowd that they were brought back and clothed in loose gowns. The cow threw Perpetua to the ground, tearing her dress, and she sat up and drew it about her, "being more mindful of shame than of pain"; and she tidied her hair, "lest its dishevelment should make it appear that a martyr mourned in her glory". Then she went to help Felicity, who also had been tossed, and together they were called back out of the arena.

The whole group, after having kissed one another, "that their martyrdom might be perfected with the rite of peace", was eventually slain by the sword. All died without sound or movement, except Perpetua: her executioner was a novice, and his first clumsy blow drew a shriek from her; "and when his unpractised hand still wavered, she herself guided the sword to her throat".

The account written by and of these martyrs[1] has the same lyric vibrancy that is found in St Ignatius's letter to the Roman Christians, modified by a certain feminine reticence. It shows the same heroic love for God that leads to a total giving up

[1] The whole thing is translated by W. H. Shewring, with a Latin text, in *The Passion of SS. Perpetua and Felicity* (London, 1931). There are several other English versions.

of self, involving in the case of the women the sacrifice of loved
ones too, a father, children. The whole of human affection is
made a burnt-offering, so nobly—and so simply.

## ST ANTONY AND THE DESERT FATHERS

In the year 270 a twenty-year-old Egyptian, Antony by name,
lost his parents. They had brought him up a good Christian,
and he and his younger sister inherited from them a considerable estate in land between Lake Moeris and the Nile. But
Antony had heard a call: "If thou hast a mind to be perfect,
go home and sell all that belongs to thee; give it to the poor,
and so the treasure thou hast shall be in heaven; then come
back and follow me" (Matt. 19. 21). Accordingly, he provided
for his sister, distributed his land, and sold the rest of his goods
for the benefit of the poor.

In those days there were not yet any proper monasteries in
Egypt, so Antony turned to an old hermit, asking that he might
be trained by him in the ascetic life: manual work, prayer,
searching of the Scriptures. At once he had, for the first time,
to undergo severe temptations: longing for the easy life he
had given up, remorse for having left his sister, anticipated
dislike of the monotonous life he had undertaken, repeated
assaults of sensuality and enticing imaginings. It was the first
phase of a conflict that was to last for over seventy years.
Strong in Christ, Antony redoubled his austerities, eating only
a little bread, fasting from all food sometimes for days on end,
sleeping on a rush-mat or on the bare ground. Wanting more
solitude, and, as it were, to chase the Devil to his lair, he took
up his quarters in an empty tomb, one of those numerous
burial-caves in the cliffs of the Nile valley, where a friend
brought him supplies of food from time to time. Here the conflict became fiercer than ever; it was reputed that evil spirits
were especially given to haunting lonely spots and burial-
places.

Some years later, when he was thirty-five, Antony went still farther into the wilderness, crossing to the desert on the eastern side of the Nile. He found the ruins of a deserted fort, which he had first to clear of snakes. He rebuilt the enclosing wall, and now his friend had to throw food over it to him inside. He lived here for twenty years. But his example was contagious, and many Christians wanted to live a similar life of prayer and hardship. They came and asked him to be their guide, and so it came about that Antony established two "monasteries", one on either side of the river. They were, in fact, simply groups of huts or cells, each with one occupant, and there was no written rule of life. Antony did no more than give them example and advice—how to progress in love for God, how to drive off evil spirits.

In the year 311 Antony went for a time to Alexandria, to succour the victims of persecution under the emperor Maximinus, seeking them out in their prisons and in the labour-camps at the mines. Later, his monasteries multiplied and visitors gave him no time to devote to God, so he fled to the south in quest of solitude. Joining a caravan of "Saracens", Beduin Arabs, he travelled three days and nights in the hill country between the Nile and the Red Sea, till he found a little oasis, a spring of water and a few date-palms. Here he settled down. He gave himself wholly to prayer and study of the Bible, increasing his fasting and night-watches and other austerities, so that his mind and spirit became ever more taken up with God. He lived thus in this place for forty years, dying in 356 at the age of 105 years.

Not long before his death Antony went to visit his disciples around the Nile, and he again visited Alexandria, to help its bishop, St Athanasius, in his troubles with the Arians. But such journeys were unusual; Antony's admirers, and they were many, had to come to him, along desert ways and mountain tracks. For the last fifteen years of his life he allowed two of his followers, Macarius and Amathas, to live near him.

St Antony had no other aim than to overcome the world and live with God; but in fact it was he who started that great monastic movement that peopled the Egyptian deserts with religious solitaries and communities during the fourth century; from thence it spread to Palestine, Cappadocia, Italy and Gaul, and saved the whole Church from decline.[1]

## ST AUGUSTINE OF HIPPO

Augustine was nearly thirty-three when he was baptized at Milan in 387. His mother was a Christian, and at his birth he was signed with the cross, and he received the salt of a catechumen; but his baptism was put off, for fear that when he grew up he might repudiate the promises made in his name.

He was an African, of enthusiastic and passionate temperament and of searching intelligence, driven by a desire to understand everything, eager of heart, in love with love. First at his birthplace and then at Carthage he was a painstaking, brilliant student; but he lived very loosely. "In youth I was burning to gorge myself with wicked sensuality," he wrote afterwards, "and I was not ashamed to delight myself first with one woman and then another" (*Confessions*, ii, 2). Eventually he entered into a stable relationship with a woman who bore him a son; he brought the child up and was greatly attached to him.

But an irregular life did not put an end to Augustine's studies, and the *Hortensius* of Cicero turned his mind to philosophy. An attempt to study the Christian sacred books had come to nothing: the young rhetor was put off by their simple forthrightness. Then he fell into Manichaeism, whose teaching seemed to explain the twofold attraction by which he was torn: on the one hand, mind and spirit were drawn to that sovereign Beauty which the Christ of his childhood and his philosophical reflections had revealed to him; on the other, his heart was enslaved to disordered passion. Manichaeism put the powers of good and of evil on the same level, and locked them in a struggle that neither could win: it took Augustine nine years to free himself from that teaching.

[1] The classical Life of St Antony is by St Athanasius. The latest English version is in the Ancient Christian Writers series, No. 10.

During those years his profession as teacher of rhetoric and grammar had taken him from Thagaste, where he was born, to Carthage, then to Rome and finally to Milan, where he hoped to get a good post (Milan was then the imperial residence). It was there that he found a master, in its bishop, St Ambrose, whose eloquence captivated Augustine; it was Ambrose who opened to him those treasures of the Bible that once had repelled him. Mentally he was ready to accept the Christian faith, but the flesh held him back: "I said within myself, 'Make an end, make an end!' I nearly came to a resolve, but did not. . . . The nearer I came to being another man, the more repelled I was. . . . What held me back was my old trouble, those vanities of vanities, the mistresses I had had, who plucked at my fleshly robe and whispered softly, 'Are you sending us away? Shall we never be with you again? Is this and that now forbidden to you?' " (*op. cit.*, xi, 25–6).

The grace of God that had pursued him for so long conquered at this critical moment. For eight months he prepared for baptism, giving up his school and retiring to a house near Milan. The "new man" was coming to birth.

Soon after his baptism, Augustine returned to Africa, where he hoped for the future to lead with some friends a sort of monastic life of prayer and intellectual work. But his fellow citizens would not allow it. The aged bishop of Hippo needed an assistant, the people clamoured that Augustine should be the man, and in 391 he was ordained priest. Two years later he was made bishop, and succeeded to the see of Hippo in 396. He was bishop there for thirty-four years.

During the first part of his life St Augustine was seeking God gropingly, here and there, through a variety of experiences. During the second part, having found him at last, he devoted all his time and all his powers to him. He no longer belonged to himself. In the first place he belonged to the people of Hippo, whose father he was and whose every soul it was his responsibility to lead to God. But it was not this little diocese alone, it was the church of North Africa and the whole universal Church that claimed his days and nights. It was no longer a matter of distinguishing himself to show off his eloquence to better advantage. He had only one concern now: by word and deed, by writing and by apostleship, ceaselessly to serve the God who from henceforth was his only love.[1]

## ST SIMEON AND THE PILLAR SAINTS

Less than a century after the death of St Antony solitaries and cenobites were numerous, not only in Egypt and Palestine, but also in Syria. It was there, near Antioch, that, about the year 402, a youth named Simeon began to lead an ascetical life. He sought to bring his body into subjection by increasingly severe austerities, particularly by most alarming fasting. One Lent he determined to eat nothing at all, and he asked to be shut up in a cell for this purpose; this was agreed, but on condition that some bread and water should be left with him. When the cell was opened at the end of the forty days, Simeon was found to be only just alive, but the bread and water were untouched. He repeated this every Lent for the rest of his life.

By the time he was thirty-four, people were flocking to Simeon to seek his prayers and advice, and, hoping thereby to escape their importunities, he had the idea of living on the top of a pillar. He began with one about nine feet high, and gradually increased the height till it was sixty feet, and at this height he passed the last twenty or so years of his life. The base of this column is still in existence, standing amid the ruins of a basilica that was built around it soon after Simeon's death. It was surmounted by the platform on which he lived, which is calculated to have measured about twelve feet square. There was no shelter on it, but it was surrounded by a balustrade and in the middle was a post to which Simeon sometimes tied himself during his lenten fast. Ordinarily he stood upright, exposed to

[1] A contemporary Life of St Augustine is translated in F. R. Hoare's *The Western Fathers* (London and New York, 1954). His *Confessions* have been translated by F. J. Sheed (London and New York, 1944).

the fierce Syrian sun and to every other weather, praying by day and by night and constantly making deep reverences or prostrations. From three in the afternoon until sunset he was at people's disposal, teaching, exhorting, answering questions. He was a very friendly man, full of kindly sympathy and common sense in his advice (he urged moneylenders not to charge more than six per cent. interest).

Simeon's fame extended far beyond the frontiers of Syria, and people travelled long distances to consult him. The Arabs came in hundreds, and there were many conversions. He was known even in the West: the monk who wrote the Life of St Geneviève of Paris at the beginning of the sixth century records that she and St Simeon used to pray for one another.

Simeon died on his pillar in 459, his death not being discovered till two days later; he was seventy years old, and had been a stylite for thirty-seven of them. The particulars related above are not legendary: they are attested by authentic and contemporary documents. St Simeon made such an impression that after he was dead not a few others copied his way of life; but it was not taken up in the West.[1]

## ST FRANCIS OF ASSISI

As a young man Francis gave up the comfortable life of a wealthy merchant's son in order more closely to follow Jesus, especially in his poverty; with his companions he lived by the work of his hands and, when need be, on alms. Here are two passages from the *Little Flowers of St Francis* which show how extreme austerity was combined in him with cheerfulness and joy. In the first he tells his friend Brother Leo how happiness is to be found in utter destitution.

If when we reach St Mary of the Angels we are soaked with rain, frozen with cold, filthy with mud and ravenous with

---

[1] For further particulars of St Simeon Stylites the Elder, and of other pillar-saints, such as Simeon the Younger and Daniel of Constantinople, see the revised edition of Butler's *Lives of the Saints* (4 vols., London and New York, 1956).

hunger; and if when we knock, the doorkeeper comes angrily and says, "Who are you?" and we say, "We are two of your brethren", and he answers, "You lie. You are a couple of rascals who go about cheating people and stealing alms from the poor: go away!"; and if he will not open the door, but makes us stay outside all night, hungry and cold in the snow and rain: why then, if we are patient, and put up with such unkindness and abuse and rebuffs without complaint or murmuring, and believe humbly and charitably that the doorkeeper really knows us but God makes him turn us away—then, brother Leo, write down that *there* is perfect joy. (Ch. viii.)

In the second passage, poverty wears a less frowning face. Brother Francis and Brother Masseo are journeying towards France.

One day they came to a town and, being very hungry, they begged bread for love of God according to the Rule, St Francis taking one street and Brother Masseo another. But, being a little man, not much to look at, people who did not know him were contemptuous of St Francis, and he collected only a few mouthfuls of stale crust; whereas Brother Masseo, who was tall and good-looking, was given plenty of good bread.

Outside the town was a pleasant spring of water, and when they had begged their food they met here, spreading out what they had collected on a fine large rock. When St Francis saw how much more and better Brother Masseo's bread was than his, he said gaily, "We do not deserve such treasure, Brother Masseo." He repeated these words several times, till Brother Masseo remarked, "How can that be called treasure, dear father, when all is so poor and so much is lacking? There is no table-cloth or knife or plate or bowl or house or table or waiter or maid."

To that St Francis answered: "That is just what seems to me great treasure: where nothing is prepared for us by human hands but all by divine providence, as we see in the bread we have begged, this fine stone table and this sparkling spring. So let us pray God that he may make us wholeheartedly love this noble treasure of holy poverty with which he himself serves us." When he had said this, they made their prayer and refreshed their bodies on the bread and water; this done, they rose to their feet and went on towards France. (Ch. xiii.)

The same spirit shines in the *Song of Brother Sun*, which Francis spoke at the moment when life was ebbing from his worn-out body.

> Most high, all-mighty, all-good Lord,
> Yours be the praise, the glory, honour and
>     all blessing!
> To you alone, most High, are they due,
> And no man is worthy to name your Name.
>
> Praise to you, Lord, with all your creatures,
> Especially Brother Sun,
> Who at your word gives day to lighten us.
> He is glorious, and his shining splendour
> Signifies you, most High!
> And praise to you, Lord, for our Sister Moon and
>     Sisters Stars
> Set in the heavens by you,
> Precious and clear and lovely.
>
> Praise to you, Lord, for Brother Wind,
> And air and clouds, good weather and all weather,
> By which you give your creatures sustenance.
> Praise to you, Lord, for Sister Water,
> The useful, humble, pure and cleansing.
> Praise to you, Lord, for Brother Fire,
> The strong and joyful, fierce and beauteous,
> By whom you lighten darkness.
> Praise to you, Lord, for our sister and our
>     mother, Earth,
> Who feeds and strengthens us
> And brings forth fruit and coloured flowers
>     and trees....
>
> May all things praise and bless the Lord,
> And give him thanks and serve him humbly![1]

[1] The *Little Flowers* (*Fioretti*) has often been translated into English. One of the best lives of St Francis in any language is that by Father Cuthbert of Brighton, Capuchin (London, 1925).

## ST LOUIS OF FRANCE

King Louis IX of France was everything good that we understand by the term "knightly", as is made abundantly clear in the account written of him by his comrade-in-arms John of Joinville.

At the landing of the crusaders in Egypt in 1249, "When the King heard that the ensign of St Denis was ashore he strode across the galley, refusing even for the Legate who was with him to lag behind the standard, and leapt into the water, which came up to his armpits. His shield round his neck, his helmet on his head, lance in hand, he joined his men on the beach" (Ch. xxxv). Some weeks later, in the Nile delta, "while I was on foot with my knights, wounded, as I have already told you, up came the King with his own division; there was a great shouting and a tremendous noise of trumpets and kettledrums; he halted on a raised roadway. Never have I seen so fine a man in arms; he towered head and shoulders over his people, a gilded helmet on his head, and in his hand a sword of German steel" (Ch. xlvii).

After defeat, sickness, capture and ransoming, Louis landed at Akka on the coast of Palestine, a fortified town still in crusading hands. On a Sunday he sent for his brothers and the other nobles to discuss his possible return to France: the queen-mother had recalled him, for his kingdom was in danger. If he left Palestine, however, the country would be lost, for no crusader would want to stay there after he had gone. Louis gave his followers a week to think about it, and on the following Sunday they met again. The barons were for evacuation; there had been eighteen hundred knights, and they were now not more than about a hundred: it would be better, they said, to go back to France and fit out a new expedition. Joinville himself was the fourteenth to give his opinion. He spoke out boldly and declared that, since the king still had some forces, he could carry on the campaign for another year; this would enable them to rescue prisoners who otherwise would never be free again. Louis said he would give his decision in another week's time.

When we came out they began to attack me on all sides. "My Lord of Joinville, the King must indeed be out of his mind if he prefers your advice to that of the whole Council of the Kingdom of France." When the tables were set, the King bade me sit by him at dinner, in the place he always gave me when his brothers were absent. All during dinner he did not speak a word to me, though it was his usual custom to be free with me at table. I thought, indeed, that he was angry with me for saying that he had not yet spent any of his own money and that he should not be sparing of it.

While the King was hearing grace I went to a barred window in an alcove by the head of the King's bed. I passed my arms through the bars and was thinking that if the King returned to France I should follow the advice the Lord of Bourlemont gave me and go to the Prince of Antioch (who counted me a kinsman and had sent for me) until I could join another expedition or peace was confirmed and the prisoners released.

As I stood there, the King came and leant on my shoulders and put his two hands on my head. I thought it was my Lord Philip of Nemours, who had already tormented me a great deal that day on account of the advice I had given the King. "Leave me in peace, my Lord Philip," I said. It happened, as I turned my head, that the King's hand slipped down in front of my face, and I recognized him by an emerald he wore on his finger. "Keep quite still," he said. "I want to ask you something: how could a young man like you be so bold as to advise me to stay, in the face of all the great and wise of France who told me to go?"

"Sir," I said, "even if I had that evil thought in my heart, I would never at any price have given you such advice." "Do you mean," he said, "that I should do wrong to leave?" "God help me, sir, I do." Then he added, "If I stay, will you also stay?" I told him that I would, either at my own or at another's charges. "Be easy, then," he said, "for I am indeed pleased by your advice. But say no word of it to any man during this week."

When the next Sunday came round, Louis announced that his brothers should return to France but that he would stay.

This great king (who was father of eleven children) was intransigent about his royal prerogatives; but he used to get up at midnight to be at Matins in his chapel, he assisted at Mass twice every morning and at the Divine Office during the day, and he did not go to bed till he had said the angel's salutation to Mary half a hundred times. To those who thought he was "too pious", he replied that nobody would complain if he spent twice as much time dicing or hunting.

Every day he had a hundred and more poor people fed, and twice as many on feast-days, when he waited on them himself in his castle. He had a number of hospitals built, wherein he himself sometimes tended the sick, however repellent their diseases; Joinville relates how, in Egypt, St Louis would carry rotting corpses to burial, without showing disgust at the task as others did. Throughout his reign he laboured for justice in his kingdom and to maintain peace among Christian princes. Death, from typhus, took him near Tunis on August 25th, 1270, while he was on a last crusade; on the night before he died he was heard to say, "We are going to Jerusalem."

St Louis had sought the earthly Jerusalem, not in order to beat the infidels in battle, but in the hope of converting them to Christ, so that they might share with him the grace he had received in babyhood at the font at Poissy.[1]

## ST TERESA OF AVILA

When this lively and good-looking Castilian girl of noble birth became a Carmelite nun, at the age of twenty, it was not in any access of religious enthusiasm. She wrote later on: "I remember that when I left my father's house I suffered so much that I do not believe I can suffer more when I come to die; it seemed as if every bone of my body was wrenched apart, and that love for God would never outweigh love for my father and

[1] The best of several English translations of Joinville's memoirs is René Hague's *The Life of St Louis* (London and New York, Sheed & Ward, 1955). The quotations above are taken from this.

relatives. I felt this so strongly that all my reasons would not have induced me to go on with it if the Lord had not come to my help. God gave me such courage against myself at that time that I carried out my determination" (*Autobiography*, ch. iv).

Neither was she persuaded to it by her family. Her mother had been dead seven years, and her father opposed her going into the convent. But from her childhood Teresa had learned from reading saints' lives that life without heroism is not worth much, and, while her brothers enlisted for the conquest of the New World, she enlisted in the service of the King of kings.

Unhappily the life of the Carmel of the Incarnation that she joined did not conduce to an heroic life. There were 180 nuns in it, who lived under a mitigated rule that allowed them much liberty and a certain comfort. There Teresa was to pass twenty-seven years, during the first twenty of which she failed to find a confessor capable of understanding and directing her. Apart from an occasional short moment of intense contemplation, these were years of spiritual dryness. They were, moreover, broken by two years of nervous illness, followed by a convalescence outside the convent walls. She then returned to a monastic life that was open to worldly influences. "On one hand, God was calling me; on the other, I was following the world. The things of God gave me happiness, but those of the world had a hold on me. It looked as if I wanted to reconcile opposites, to bring these contradictory things together: the life of the spirit with the satisfactions, pleasures and amusements of the senses. I passed many years thus . . ." (*op. cit.*, ch. viii). But it must be noticed that, in spite of aridity, she had for ten years been faithful to mental prayer and meditation.

St Teresa was nearly forty years old when she finally and completely rejected compromise. "From then on I turned over a new leaf and led another, new life. Till then, it was a matter of my own life for myself: thenceforward, it was God's life in me" (*op. cit.*, ch. xxiii). From the moment that she gave herself wholly to divine grace, God began to lavish the gifts of mystical life upon her. She has given a minutely detailed account of their stages, in the books she wrote under obedience to her superiors' request and for the instruction of those who in their turn should be called to such remarkable oneness with God. Teresa was bewildered by the extraordinary graces that she received: ecstasies, raptures, divine communications, visions. She received guidance among these unprecedented experiences from excellent confessors, who were able to assure her of their divine origin. But it was difficult for Teresa to lead her new life in the convent of the Incarnation. So after eight years she was authorized to found a little community which, in complete poverty, lived according to the strict rule of the old Carmelite houses. This was her first foundation, in 1562.

That was the beginning of the reform of Carmel that St Teresa was to carry on for twenty years, in the course of which she successfully made eighteen new foundations all over Spain. Nor did her own inner life suffer harm from her astounding activity: constant travelling, maddeningly difficult negotiations with civil and ecclesiastical authorities, worries about building and organization, the responsibilities of administration and religious guidance, a huge correspondence, and the writing of books that are still masterpieces of Spanish literature as well as a *vade-mecum* of the contemplative life. And she did and looked after all this with unfailing sense of humour, wit, distinction, high-mindedness, delicacy of perception and womanly charm!

When death was at hand and she was about to receive her *viaticum*, St Teresa exclaimed, "Bridegroom and Lord, the longed-for hour has come! It is time for us to see one another, my Beloved, my Master. It is time for me to set out. Let us go. . . ."[1]

[1] There are translations of St Teresa's *Autobiography* by David Lewis (reprinted in U.S.A., 1943) and by E. A. Peers (London and New York, 1946).

## ST THOMAS MORE

By the time he was forty, Thomas More was the most celebrated lawyer in London and a member of King Henry VIII's
council. Among his friends was one of the greatest scholars of
the Renaissance, Erasmus of Rotterdam, who in 1519 wrote a
description of More in a famous letter to Ulrich von Hutten.
After describing his physical appearance and habits (he was
a water-drinker, detested gambling, was fond of music), Erasmus goes on:

He is so charming and cheerful in daily life that he can make
the most solemn people smile and lighten the most disagreeable
situation. From childhood he was so fond of witticisms that he
seemed to have been born simply to make them. . . .

He finds entertainment in every human contact, however
momentous the occasion. When he is with scholars, their learning delights him; with fools, he laughs at their folly. Lunatic
chatter does not upset him, for he knows exactly how to adapt
himself to anything. With women, including his wife, he is
nearly always joking. . . . He is very fond of animals, and
watches every aspect of them closely. All the birds come to him
to be fed, and he keeps less common creatures too—a monkey,
a fox, a ferret, a weasel. Whenever he sees anything out of the
way, he buys it: his house is a regular museum; and every
visitor can find something of interest in it, and their interest
doubles his pleasure.

In his time he has not been indifferent to the attractions of
young women. . . . He was quite young when he began to study
Greek and philosophy. . . . When he had made trial of the
schools, he turned to law, and became so proficient that there
was no one with a better practice. . . . He studied divinity,
too . . . , priests and experienced men were not ashamed to
learn from this young layman. . . . He was zealous in religion,
and prepared for [possible] priesthood by vigil, fast and
prayer. . . . Nothing stood in the way of his entering a monastery
[he had thought of being a Carthusian], but desire for marriage
drew him the other way. He would rather be a chaste husband
than a vicious priest.

So he married a girl [Jane Colt] of good birth who had lived all her life with her family in the country. She was quite uneducated, and he was able to bring her up according to his own ideas. He taught her books and music, and looked forward to passing the rest of his life with her. But she died before her time, after bearing several children. . . . He was not meant to be a celibate; against the advice of his friends he very soon married again, a widow, less for love than to have someone to look after his family. He used to say with a laugh that she was neither young nor pretty, but she was a careful housewife and a good mother to the children. He was as considerate and affectionate towards her as if she had been glowing with youth and beauty. . . .

. . . He is fervently religious, and quite free from superstition. His prayers are not drawn from set forms, but come from the promptings of his spirit. When he talks with his friends about the life to come, you feel that what he says springs from a heart that is full of hope.

What Erasmus did not say—he did not know it—was that this fastidious humanist, this hospitable host who enjoyed life, this seeming amateur of good things, was the wearer of a hairshirt.

Ten years after the date of this letter, in 1529, King Henry appointed More to one of the most responsible and important posts in the kingdom, the lord-chancellorship. The king was very fond of him and knew his great prestige with everybody, and he hoped to get More's approval for the matter then filling his mind—the nullity of his marriage with Katherine of Aragon, which Rome was opposing.

For nearly three years More endeavoured to hold back his sovereign from schism. But when he saw his efforts were fruitless and that he would be expected to approve the king's assumption of the headship of the Church in England, he resigned the lord chancellor's office. This reduced him and his household to a state bordering on poverty. Wood fuel could no longer be afforded in winter: all the family sat round a fire of bracken stalks, and went to bed no better warmed than that.

After the "divorce" and Henry's marriage to Anne Boleyn, More did not attend the new queen's coronation. Eighteen months later the king appointed a committee to examine More on certain charges of treason brought against him. After the interview, his son-in-law, William Roper, said to him, "I trust, sir, that all is well, because you are so merry." To which More replied: "In good faith, I rejoiced, son, that I had given the devil a foul fall, and that with those lords I had gone so far as without great shame I could never go back again."

More had written to the king, reminding him that, when he resigned the chancellorship, "it pleased your Highness further to say unto me, that for the service which before I had done you . . . in any suit that I should after have to your Grace, that either should concern mine honour (that word it liked your Highness to use unto me), or that should pertain unto my profit, I should find your Highness good and gracious lord to me". He then goes on:

> So it is now, gracious Sovereign, that worldly honour is the thing whereof I have resigned both the possession and the desire, in the resignation of your most honourable office; and worldly profit I trust experience proveth, and daily more and more shall prove, that I never was very greedy thereon. But now is my most humble suit unto your excellent Highness . . . that . . . no sinister information move your noble Grace to have any more distrust of my truth and devotion toward you than I have or shall during my life give the cause. . . . I only beseech your Majesty . . . consider and weigh the matter . . . and that if, in your so doing, your own virtuous mind shall give you that . . . I be a wretch of such a monstrous ingratitude . . . then desire I no further favour at your gracious hand than the loss of all that ever I may lose, goods, lands, liberty, and my life withal, whereof the keeping of any part unto myself could never do me pennyworth of pleasure. But only should my comfort be, that after my short life and your long . . . I should once meet your Grace and be merry again with you in heaven, where, among mine other pleasures, this should yet be one, that your Grace should surely see there then that, howsoever you take me, I am

your true bedesman now, and ever have been, and will be till I die, howsoever your pleasure be to do by me.

Within a few weeks an oath was tendered to More which he could not in conscience take, and he was imprisoned in the Tower of London. He was there over a year, lodged in a cold cell where he lived like a Carthusian monk such as he had once wanted to be. At his trial he conducted his defence with fine acumen, quietly and good-humouredly, as in the days when he had practised law. All he need have done to be set free was to acknowledge the king's spiritual headship; he rejected it, categorically but without defiance: to have done otherwise would have been to go against his conscience, to deny Christ's Church, to love life more than God. He was condemned to death.

Thomas More was executed on July 6th, 1535, and he entertained death as he had formerly entertained his friends, courteously, gaily, with smiling gentleness. At the scaffold on Tower Hill he joked with the lieutenant: "I pray you, master lieutenant, see me safe up, and for my coming down let me shift for myself." He spoke a few words to the people, asking their prayers, and declaring that he died in and for the faith of the Catholic Church, "the king's good servant, but God's first". He knelt and said the psalm *Miserere*, and kissed the headsman, saying to him, "Pluck up thy spirits, man, and be not afraid to do thine office; my neck is very short, take heed therefore thou strike not awry, for saving of thine honesty." At the block he bound his eyes himself and adjusted his beard ("It has not committed treason")—we are reminded of Perpetua tidying her hair in the arena at Carthage.[1]

## ST VINCENT DE PAUL

If anything should be added to St Paul's famous encomium of charity it should perhaps be "Charity is enterprising, con-

[1] The best recent lives of St Thomas More are those by R. W. Chambers (London, 1935, Westminster, Md., 1949) and E. E. Reynolds (London and New York, 1953).

triving and systematic". The charity of St Vincent de Paul was certainly these things.

He was thirty years old when divine charity captured his heart, and for half a century thereafter his passionate love of God and his neighbour in God gave him no rest. That love prompted him to undertakings that a man of mundane genius would not even have thought of; it stirred his solid good sense and peasant tenacity to work them out in detail and to develop them fearlessly. When he died in his eightieth year in 1660, he had built up a prodigious edifice of good works and prepared yet greater harvests for ages to come.

When he was ordained priest at the uncanonically early age of twenty, Vincent de Paul seems to have had no other aim than to lead a quiet ecclesiastical life of respectable ease. But divine grace was at work. Apparently Vincent's acquaintance with the holy Father Peter de Bérulle counted for a lot in his conversion. For three or four years he was very much disturbed by distressing temptations against faith; and it was when he emerged from this ordeal that he committed himself to a faithful following of Jesus Christ by dedicating the whole of his life to the service of the poor. From then on charitable works appear one by one, at first in a small way but soon organized to grow and become permanent.

Thus in 1617, when for a few months he was ministering in a parish to the north of Lyons, he mentioned to the congregation one Sunday a family living in a remote place every one of whose members was ill. After Vespers he went to call on them himself, and on the way he met several ladies going to or coming from the same destination; it at once occurred to him that they should use their benevolent energies more economically: "I suggest to these good people whom charity has prompted to go there that they should get together and arrange to look after this family on different days of the week, and to care for others as well."

That is how the first Confraternity of Charity began. After

three months' experience its rules were drawn up in detail; here
is a passage from them:

> The person whose turn it is to provide dinner will take it to
> those who are sick, and greet them cheerfully and kindly.
> Arrange the little table for the bed, with a cloth, cup, spoon
> and some bread. Wash the patient's hands, and say grace. Pour
> the soup into a bowl and put the meat on a plate, and arrange
> them on the table. Then gently invite the patient to eat, in the
> name of Jesus and of his holy Mother. Do everything lovingly,
> as if it were for your own child, or rather, for God, who takes
> what is done for the poor as done for himself. Say a word or
> two about our Lord to the sick person, thus seeking to cheer
> him up if he be dejected; cut up his food, and pour out his
> drink. Then, when everything is ready for the meal and if there
> be anyone else there, go away and find the next one to be
> looked after in the same fashion. Always remember to begin
> with those who have somebody with them, so that you will be
> able to have more time for those who are alone.

Within a few years there were charitable groups of this kind
in fifteen Parisian parishes and in numerous towns and villages.

St Vincent's other foundations came about in a similar way,
as circumstances arose, and they flourished from the moment
that they caught something of the burning spirit of his love.

The Ladies of Charity could not give all their time to the
sick, so Monsieur Vincent had the idea of enlisting the help of
young women who could devote their whole time to the work.
Thus were born the Daughters of Charity, who today are called
the Sisters of Charity of St Vincent de Paul. At the time of his
death they already numbered over a thousand: today there are
forty-three thousand of them.

In those days four or five hundred children were left forsaken
in the streets of Paris every year. Monsieur Vincent resolved
to take charge of them, and won over the Ladies of Charity
to the cause, for the expense involved was enormous. Later,
King Louis XIV in Paris and Captain Thomas Coram in
London established their foundling hospitals, and eventually

public authorities in various countries woke up to their responsibilities.

When Lorraine, Artois, Picardy, Champagne and elsewhere were ravaged by war, Monsieur Vincent was able to send help in all directions. The lieutenant-general of Saint-Quentin wrote to him in 1655: "During the past week we have had as many as 1,400 miserable refugees in this town in the wake of the troops: thanks to your help, they have been fed every day. As well as these from the country, there is another 1,000 or more who are relying solely on your charity for food."

Monsieur Vincent's efforts on behalf of galley-slaves, beggars, decayed gentry and the aged are well known. There is no human suffering that he did not seek to relieve; his missioners reached the poor and oppressed so far away as Ireland, Scotland and the Hebrides themselves. It is astonishing how he was able to inspire so much good will and to collect so much money through pure generosity.

Yet all this is only one aspect of his charitable activity. His genius was no less exercised on behalf of the spiritually needy, and he used the same bold and wise methods.

The confession of a dying man whom he had converted showed him the need for missioners to the countryside. He began with a few priests, who were the origin of the Congregation of the Mission (Vincentians, or Lazarists).

The good that missioners can do is soon wasted if there be not a good parochial clergy. But in those days most priests were ordained after no other preparation than a university education. Monsieur Vincent started by organizing retreats of a fortnight in order to give ordinands a minimum spiritual preparation for their ministry. But what is a fortnight in the training of a priest? It was seminaries that were wanted. With the Oratorians and with Monsieur Olier at Saint-Sulpice, Vincent de Paul was one of those to whom the Church owes the spread of these necessary institutions.

However well trained he may be, the priest has still to keep his spiritual life going healthily. For this purpose Monsieur Vincent established the Tuesday Conferences for the clergy of Paris. And for ten years he was a member of the royal commission whose duty it was to choose candidates for the French episcopate.

St Vincent de Paul approached each of his undertakings, however important, with that same humbleness and simplicity that made him exclaim at each success, "I did not think it out. God thought it out for us."[1]

[1] Mgr J. Calvet's *St Vincent de Paul* has been translated by L. C. Sheppard (London and New York, 1952).

# CHAPTER III

# THE SPIRIT OF THE SAINTS

At the end of Chapter I we said that there is not a difference of kind but only of degree between those we now call saints and the general run of those who make up the "holy people". We will now use the examples just given to make a comparison between authentic saints and the indifferent members of the holy people that we are. The differences that we shall find will bring into relief some of the characteristics of the spirit and soul of the saints. We shall then be able to compare them with people we admire because of their spiritual worth but who are not Christians. This comparison too will help us to see more exactly what holiness really is.

## THEY HAVE FAITH

For a person to be sanctified by baptism he must have faith. But, alas! how many baptized people have a faith that is hardly more than verbal?

Compare their conviction about things seen (the existence of the sun, of their house, of their children) with their conviction about things unseen (life after death, the presence of Christ in the Eucharist and in their souls, or even simply the existence of a personal God who reads their thoughts). About the first they are absolutely certain, with a certainty that involves their whole being; for the second they have a good-willed acquiescence, which does not go much deeper than a recital of the words of the Creed and has no hold on their fundamental reactions. Studying these reactions, try to compare the two certainties that they have, or ought to have, at a time of bereavement: I know that my child is dead, I know that his soul is living with God. They must not be blamed for being so overwhelmed; that is understandable enough. But can one really speak of faith?

One of the first reasons for the alarming proportion of feeble Christians is that they have hardly got faith. They are nevertheless part of the holy people, in name at any rate, and we hope that they will not be excluded from it in the day of judgement. But their holiness is compromised by their quasi-unbelievingness.

Real saints on the other hand, such people as those of whom we have given some instances, believe wholly and completely in the invisible realities of their *Credo*. Their belief is not a matter of words recited energetically: they know and attend to the meaning of those words, and in practice hold the meaning to be as true as the things they know on the evidence of their senses. When St Ignatius of Antioch and St Louis said that they believed in everlasting life they were not repeating a formula: their whole existence was given up to that certainty.

Some saints have had temptations against faith, to the verge of doubt, and suffered horribly in consequence. But their very sufferings are evidence of how important faith was to them: all their love, their whole reason for living, was at stake. Half-believers know no such crises. Their belief is only on the surface, and if they lose the little faith they have there will be no appreciable difference in the way that they live.

It must not be forgotten that faith is not simply an intellectual matter. The assent of the understanding is given under the impulsion of grace and with the cooperation of the will.

## COURAGE TO CHOOSE

If the mass of baptized had a stronger faith they would appreciate what their baptism commits them to and they would have the courage to *choose*. In principle they have chosen Christ, but they are always going back on their choice. They are afraid to take sides. And that is why, through reaction, their faith is not firmer, for, as we have just recalled, it largely depends on the will.

The "middling" Christian is afraid to commit himself and to make a choice because to choose is to sacrifice. We cannot be indwelt by the spirit of Christ and the spirit of the world both at the same time. If we choose Christ we have to give up the world and the three-faced devil that steers it: the spirit of greed and of pleasure and of pride. The feeble Christian tries to live at least at the edge of the world, so as not to have to give up all his pleasures but without losing Christ. He is like the bad gambler who plays at two tables at once.

The saints rejected these half-measures and compromises, because they loved. The obvious case is that of the martyrs. They were faced by a clear alternative, and they had to make their choice willy-nilly: either Christ, by way of death, or life, by way of disowning him. Ignatius, Perpetua and Felicity, Thomas More sacrificed life and chose Christ—with what gallantry we have seen.

For many saints a choice is offered to rather than forced on them, for it is rare that grace takes hold of and shakes a man as it did St Paul. They find themselves faced with a choice, and they accept conversion. Some of them, such as St Augustine, give up sin and error; others, such as St Teresa and St Vincent de Paul, exchange a decent but rather worldly life for one given altogether to God. Their conflict at the moment of choice can be compared to that of the martyrs; it is sometimes perhaps just as hard. The great difficulty is that they are not forced, like the martyrs, to say Yes or No on the spot; there is the temptation to put off conversion to some future time when it may be easier. Plenty of Christians fail to be saints because they let the moment of grace slip by. Some great saints for a time ran the risk of failure by not responding to grace at once: we have referred above to Augustine's evasions and hesitations.

Grace was stronger than their weakness, and the day came when they confessed their weakness and declared that it was God who had wrought in them. But for all the rest of their lives they had to fight against backsliding into evil or lukewarmness. Conversion does not happen once for all. Every day the choice has to be confirmed, the sacrifice renewed. After their conversion saints persevere; and they go forward in holiness.

## UNIFIED LOVE

It is not often that a human being is really unified. The fact that we do not choose wholeheartedly means often that we are divided in spirit, or at any rate drawn hither and thither.

Doubtless we love God above all; but below him we love the good things he gives us and those whom he entrusts to us. We comfort ourselves with the thought that he cannot reproach us for these earthly loves, because they are "in order" and in accordance with his will. But in fact these people and things often monopolize our attention: they are uppermost in our mind and take up the greater part of our time. We cleave to God with a sincere will, and this will is dominant—at least we hope so. But it is not strong enough to draw to itself in a single whole those forces that attract us to others than him.

The saints' love for God does not prevent them from loving all around them; but it is so intense that these other loves are not only subordinate to it, they are wrapped up in and permeated by it. They do in truth love "in God". Often at their conversion they have had to sacrifice perfectly good affections because they stood in the way of a total gift of self to God. They had no intention of taking back their gift or dividing it up. They loved as much as ever, more than ever; but they loved those whom God loved and in the way he loved them, and their love for them took nothing from their mindfulness of him.

Think of St Francis' fondness for his brethren, St Teresa's for her nuns. Love for God unified their souls.

A similar concentration of all the inclinations round a dominating love is sometimes found in people who are not saints, and this love is what is called a passion. Think of a musician's passion for sound, a scholar's passion for learning, or, most obviously, a lover's passion for the beloved. Other things and persons have value in their eyes only in relation to the object of their love: if they favour that love they are good; if not, bad.

When it is said that saints love God passionately it is no adverse criticism, all the more that their passion does not make them blind to everything else, as earthly passion does in its jealousy and exclusiveness. Love "in God" wants to open itself boundlessly to all that God loves, and that means to all that is.

## GENIUS

Why when they are converted do saints give all to God? Why do they love him with so much passion? Certainly it is a matter of grace. But it is also a question of natural gifts which precede the gift of grace, and this may fitly be called their genius.

Whether it be in the field of art (Michelangelo, Beethoven) or of action (Alfred the Great) or of pure thought (Pascal), the exceptional man has to have creative power, a lively imagination, an urge to do and to do quickly, a spirited temperament. These vital forces have to be governed and ordered by reason; but if they are not there, reason will be no more than good sense.

We are not saying that saints are all men or women of genius. Some of them are indeed that. But in nearly all of them there is a deep spring of these creative, moving forces. They can never be satisfied with half-measures or what is middling; they are dauntless and impassioned. It is sometimes said of a child, "He will grow up to be a saint or a criminal", and something similar could have been applied to those whose lives we have sketched. Had grace not prompted them to a right choice or had they not responded to that grace, most of them would have followed wickedness as passionately as in fact they followed God. Given their genius, they were incapable of evading issues, of half-measures, of playing at two tables at once.

Does it follow that without these natural gifts one cannot become a saint? That the humble Christian who knows there is nothing out of the ordinary about him can therefore take refuge in the thought that God is not calling him to holiness? We must go back to what has been said before: every Christian is called to be holy, even though he is not called to be one of those leaders to whose names Christian people properly add the title Saint.

Every man has his own genius, in the sense that we have used the word; each one has been given such and such talents at birth. Everybody who knew Abbé Vianney when he was young thought that not much had been given him, and he certainly thought so himself. But nobody can know what a person is capable of until he has been given life and potentialities through grace. Abbé Vianney became St John Vianney.

## HEROISM

There is a word that sums up what distinguishes the saint from the run-of-the-mill Christian, and that word is "heroism". The saint is one who gives himself to the all-holy God heroically.

The hero has nobility of soul; he is generous; fear does not stop him; suffering does not "get him down" or death make him flinch. The hero is tenacious; he does not count the cost of attaining his goal; he will wear himself out doing it, and his strength seems more than a man's. All heroes are not saints. Pagan antiquity had them, admired them, and sang of them gloriously. Military heroism or the heroism of a mother or a husband can be found amongst unbelievers as well as amongst believers. They face danger and do not quail under hardship because they love, or because their companions in arms are counting on them, and the idea of failing them is more repugnant than suffering and death.

Love and the determination to be faithful in spite of everything is at the bottom of the heroism of the saints too. But their beloved is God, and they confront torment and death so boldly because they want to be his.

That martyrs are heroes is plain enough. Their selflessness, indeed, is often like that of military heroes, though it is more difficult to die heroically alone and forgotten in a dungeon than at the head of one's regiment. However, the martyrs usually found support in the consciousness of their responsibility towards their brethren. They knew that their example would encourage others, either to give in or to triumph. This consciousness of being a leader or a champion is one of the strongest incentives to natural heroism; it can also help supernatural heroism, whose deepest motive is the determination to refuse nothing to the God whom one loves. When the martyr accepts suffering and death rather than give his brethren an example of cowardice, it is not alone through consciousness of his duty and a sense of honour. It is because the love that fills his heart tells him that he is not to be the only one to love God. He wants his brethren to love God as he does, and with him to find their happiness in definitive union with Jesus Christ.

The same heroism is to be seen in the life of saints who are not called to the glory of martyrdom. There is a day-to-day heroism that is not less fine than the courage of him who gives his life all at once. Later on, when we come to the history of the veneration of saints, we shall see how the "confessors" and ascetics were gradually assimilated to the martyrs. And rightly, for they are inspired by the same love, and their sacrifice of life to God is not less whole, even though it has to be renewed day after day. We shall also see that, for somebody to be admitted to the calendar of the saints, the Church requires proof that he or she was virtuous in an heroic degree.

## ASCETICISM AND HOLINESS

Many saints have been exceedingly severe towards their bodies. The Desert Fathers provide examples of this just as astonishing as that of St Simeon Stylites. Indeed, among some of them there was what looks like an element of competition and "record-breaking". When St Macarius of Alexandria heard that certain monks were eating no cooked food at all during Lent, he determined to do the same all the year round; he kept it up for seven years.

Doubtless these athletes[1] of the Lord did not really intend to impress their brethren or to "show off"; there is too much evidence for their humble spirit for us to suppose that they succumbed to pride in this way. But the fact remains that their holiness did not reside in these excesses. Holiness is the quest for God, and for God alone. If bodily mortification be judged necessary in order to reach him, then it is hallowing. But if mortification itself becomes an aim and there be a danger of its being given attention for its own sake, then it is an obstacle to holiness, something that has come between God and the soul. That much said, it is hardly possible to judge the inmost motives of these giants of fasting and watching. We are poor judges in this matter: the bent of our contemporaries cannot be said to incline them to admire austere saints. They are much more attracted by those who have a smiling manner, for they seem more human. When St Antony is mentioned they at once think of St Antony of Padua; they have hardly heard of the Egyptian hermit of that name.

We are entitled to prefer a smiling saint. But we must not let that smile mislead us: it is often the expression of a spiritual integrity that could not be maintained without the spirit of penance; the gayest saints can be the most mortified. We love St Francis of Assisi because he was the friend of the sun and

---

[1] Athlete was a common term first for martyrs and then for other Christian champions. Cf. the Breviary hymn "Athleta Christi nobilis". [Trans.]

the birds, and we are charmed by his song of the creatures; but we know that he had altogether given up the pleasures those creatures could have given him. He loved them because they enabled him to give more praise to the Lord who was his only love. When he taught Brother Leo what it is that perfect joy consists in, he let us into the secret of the candour of his own soul, a candour that was due to austerity and penance. The young merchant that he once was would never have been able to sing of Brother Sun and Brother Fire in those accents, for there would have still been in him an element of selfishness that voluntary hardships had not yet got rid of.

No: saints do not look for suffering. Like all the rest of us, they have at first to inflict privations on themselves lest they give in to temptations of the senses. By voluntary penance they seek to ensure mastery of the body, so that it may not turn them from God. In this way Thomas More's hairshirt was a sort of training for the martyrdom which he did not know would one day be offered him; he wanted to make sure that, amid the world's business and the delights of humanism, he would always love and serve God first.

As saints increase in love for God it seems that mortification is not so much chosen as imposed on them by necessity. Their ever-growing consciousness of God's holiness calls for an ever-growing perfection of personal integrity; it is like a process of cleansing, through which their love for God takes them so that their progress towards him may not be slowed down in any way.

## PRAYER

Some saints are primarily contemplative, others give the greater part of their time to the Church's ministry, others again to works of apostleship and charity. But they are all men and women of prayer.

Even those whose days are taken up by pastoral duties, going about, visiting, attending to correspondence, arranging things—

they still lead their lives in the presence of God. They put aside some part of the day—or night—for recollection, to direct their thoughts to God's presence within them, to offer him all this activity in his service, to ask him to bless it and make it fruitful. It is thanks to these times of prayer, taken from the hours due to rest or sleep, that they are able to do so much without becoming atomized by their multitude of practical concerns. Some saints, such as Bernard of Clairvaux and Teresa of Avila, have had the privilege of joining an intense life of contemplation with tremendous activity, comparable with that of the most industrious and enterprising men in business or public life.

Must it be supposed that in general all saints are favoured with what are called mystical graces?[1] There is certainly a connection between growth in holiness and advance along those spiritual paths that end in mystical union. But it does not appear that this connection is such that a person's holiness can be measured by the effects of the graces of prayer that he has received. We must not confuse certain graces which God may accord (visions, ecstasies and the rest) with the grace which is God giving himself. It is this last that is sanctifying, that makes saints; and it is given in secret and cannot be seen. "Graces" may be compared to the charisms of which St Paul writes: "I may speak with every tongue that men and angels use ...", but the measure of *grace* is charity itself.

It must be remembered, too, that some temperaments are more inclined to contemplation than others. There have been many servants of God who had a very fine and wholesome mystical life, but whom the Church has not chosen to canonize; while numerous canonized saints (beginning with most of the martyrs) never attained the higher states of prayer. St Vincent de Paul was one of these, but he was a man of prayer for all that.

[1] See the volumes on mystics in this series.

## MIRACLES

"I promise you, if you have faith, though it be but like a grain of mustard seed, you have only to say to this mountain, Remove from this place to that, and it will remove . . ." (Matt. 17. 19). "I promise you, if anyone says to this mountain, Remove, and be cast into the sea, and has no hesitation in his heart, but is sure that what he says is to come about, his wish will be granted him" (Mark 11. 23).

If Christ's words about faith like a grain of mustard seed can be applied to anyone on this earth, it is surely to the saints. It is therefore to be expected that they will sometimes have had the gift of miracles.

Unfortunately their biographers have forgotten too often that a miracle, to be truly a miracle, must be something exceptional. Their admiration for their subjects has led them to record, side by side with genuine miracles, a mass of things for which there is no serious evidence or which do not necessarily require a supernatural explanation. This is a pity. An isolated miracle, if it be beyond question, is much more impressive than ten miracles of which nine are doubtful. In such an equivocal context, the authentic miracle loses its chief value, which is as a sign: God does a miracle in order to draw the attention of ordinarily inattentive eyes to the presence of the supernatural.

The Medical Bureau at Lourdes has the duty of clearing away from true miracles all those pseudo-miracles that spring up like weeds, which compromise true miracles and lessen their evidential value, even in the eyes of the faithful. It is difficult to imagine how it would have been possible to set up a medical bureau for every saint. Often enough the results would have been ridiculous. The saints themselves would have protested strongly at so much fuss being made over a few unusual things which they themselves were the first to find surprising and embarrassing.

Since there could be no official committee, the duty of discrimination fell on biographers, till such time as ecclesiastical

authority took it up in the process of beatification. It was a
difficult task. Biographers ought to have been very exacting,
examining the evidence carefully and putting down nothing
that was not certain. However, as we shall see in Chapter IX,
they generally allowed themselves to be carried away: both
because their devotion impelled them to leave out nothing that
seemed to increase the glory of their heroes, and because their
readers were avid for marvels and always wanted more. This
went on all through the Middle Ages and did not end with
them, so that it is very difficult for the historian today to pick
his way among the wonders attributed to less recent saints.

Between the realms of purely natural causes and purely
divine miracles there is an area that still awaits the proper
attention of psychologists and theologians: that of visions,
dreams, premonitions, intuitions, thought-transference and the
like. Because of their strength of personality, still more because
of the spiritual power deriving from their closeness to God, the
saints are often outstanding over those who, while not having
the saint's holiness, are given experience of these things.

When everything that is doubtful or explainable naturally
has been put aside, there remains much that is certain and
whose origin can only be supernatural. Many saints have done
miracles by the power of God. The reality of these miracles
and their meaning as signs are studied in another volume of this
series. But it must be remarked here that when God gives a
saint some extraordinary power over nature or over human
souls it is without doubt an indication of their union with him,
and so of their holiness. At the same time this power does not
itself constitute holiness. There are plenty of indubitable saints
who never wrought a miracle.

We shall see later on that the Church nowadays requires
proof of miracles, at least posthumous ones, before she canon-
izes anybody. But she interprets these miracles as supernatural
signs only after having decided that the person died a true
martyr or had lived a life of heroic virtue. If the result of the
inquiry into the heroism of his virtues had been negative, the

alleged miracles would not have been recognized as such. Heroic virtue and miracles are convergent evidences, but the second needs the corroboration of the first.

## HEALTH AND HOLINESS

In principle, holiness is independent of physical health. God's call comes to the sick as well as the healthy, and each responds to his love by turning to him with the whole self, body and soul: the healthy have to use their bodily energies in his service, the sick have to offer up to him their sufferings and disabilities. Each glorifies God in the state that divine providence has allotted to him. Nevertheless health and sickness have their effects on the spiritual condition of the saints.

First of all there are those who willingly lost their good health through the kind of life they adopted in order to be wholly given to God. St Bernard's fasting and coarse food aggravated the stomach troubles that tortured him after he went to Clairvaux; if she would not have been cured of tuberculosis, St Teresa of Lisieux would at least have lived longer if she had been treated in a better climate, instead of following the hard Carmelite rule in a cold and damp convent. Such people did not want to lose their health, as if it were something dangerous that must be given up because it bound them to the world; but they were prodigal of it, expending it freely because of their love. For them, care for physical well-being counted as nothing beside the duty of mortifying themselves and working for God.

Austerities and hard work are often less harmful to health than luxury and laziness. St Antony's great mortifications have been mentioned above, and there is contemporary evidence that he lived to be over a hundred. St Vincent de Paul worked like mad, and he was eighty when he died, in an era when people were not usually long-lived.

The fact is that saints do not look on physical health as all that important. It is a secondary good which they hardly trouble about, being concerned with the one thing necessary, to which everything secondary should be sacrificed. It is an opportune lesson for our time, when hygiene appears to be regarded as a primary virtue and the only duties some people recognize are those towards their bodies.

Another aspect of the relationship of holiness and health, or rather sickness, is found in those nervous maladies that often accompany mystical phenomena. It is very probable that a certain nervous unbalance is favourable to visions and ecstasies, as it is to poetic genius. In reverse, it is to be expected that an impassioned love of God, visited with revelations and outpourings that exceed natural forces, should have marked effects on delicate and sensitive temperaments. It is very difficult to judge exactly what is natural and what supernatural in these complex states, and to know whether an ailment is one of the causes of the states or whether it is simply a consequence of extraordinary gifts. The Church nowadays is very guarded in this matter; she is, for example, in no hurry to pronounce a case of stigmata to be miraculous.

But it must be noticed that most saints, in spite of any ailment or passing troubles, attain a state of equilibrium and mental health above that even of people who have a high degree of composure and steadiness; and this precisely because of their holiness.

The distinguished philosopher Henri Bergson, who was not formally a Christian, wrote on this subject: "Think what is achieved in the realm of deeds by such as St Paul, St Teresa, St Catherine of Siena, St Francis, St Joan of Arc and so many others. . . . When we consider to what the inner development of the great mystics led, we ask ourselves how it is possible to look on them as sick people. It is true that we all live in a state of unsteady balance, and average healthiness of mind (or of body) is a thing difficult to define. But for all that there is, exceptionally, a well-grounded healthiness of the mind that can be easily recognized. It shows itself in an inclination to do and act, in the ability to adapt oneself to circumstances, in firmness combined with flexibility, in a prophetic sense of what is possible and what is not, in a simplicity of mind that can deal with complexities, and in a very high degree of good sense" (*Les deux sources de la morale et de la religion,* p. 243). Without their holiness saints would not acquire that sturdiness of mind that Bergson admired in them.

## THE SAGE AND THE SAINT

We have been examining the question "What is a saint?" from the Christian point of view; we have set out the Church's teaching, and taken our examples from among those of the faithful whom she has canonized. But, for a better understanding of the specific nature of holiness, it is desirable also to compare the Christian saint with those who seek to develop their moral life to the level of heroism outside the Church and Christianity.

It is sometimes said of somebody who does not believe in God, or who is a religion unto himself, that he is a saint. And Christian terms are often used analogically of people some of whom were perhaps unbelievers: the English speak of the Tolpuddle Martyrs, in the cause of social justice; the French speak of the martyrs of the Resistance.

It is not a question of comparing the respective merits of great men and heroes in the Church and out of the Church; but simply of determining what characterizes the holy man among these noble examples of human worth.

Everything we have said so far shows clearly that there is no holiness without reference to God. Yet the wise man or the hero who is without God develops his personality solely through his own efforts; conscious of human nobility and trusting in the resources of his own nature, he seeks to be a man, fully a man. He knows, too, that one cannot be fully man without being generous and unselfish, and that that may one day require him to sacrifice even his life.

One may well ask if this acceptance of an obligation which may involve the giving up of life itself be not an implicit recognition of an Absolute, to which he is not yet able to give a name and which he worships without knowing it. There are people who say "I believe in God", yet their actions show that they do not believe in him. There are others who say "I do not believe in God", yet their actions are so many works of faith.

However, we are concerned here with the psychological aspect, and at this level the difference between sage and saint is that the first concentrates his attention on himself, trying to "make himself", while the second forgets himself and thinks only of God. The saint knows his own inferiority and weaknesses; but he also knows that there is present within him the God who has created him in his own image and who by grace cleanses and sanctifies that image, making it a better and better likeness. Constant living in God's presence works by making like: the soul follows the pattern of its divine environment. It is instructive to notice that the further a saint advances in heroic sanctity, the more dazzling and difficult his achievements, the more he insists that he counts for nothing and that it is God in him who is doing it all.

## CHRISTIAN SAINTS AND INDIAN MYSTICS

How do Christian saints and the mystics of India differ? The prestige of Gandhi as probably the greatest religious personality of our time forces this question on us. And the Christian West ought to see India as a standing reproach: for while the followers of Christ for the most part let themselves be led away by worldly wisdom, and strive to master physical forces for the extension of their own power, Hindu people recognize the primacy of the inner life and aim principally at the mastery of spiritual things.

For the attainment of this mastery Hindu sages subject themselves to a very severe physical discipline, called Yoga. By means of fasting, watching, bodily stillness and control of breathing, by mental concentration and restraint of the imagination, they seek to free the soul from the grip of the senses so that it may escape from the external world, the realm of illusion. Once set free, the soul will find true reality within itself, that is, God, who is everywhere and in whom the soul can be dissolved because it is of divine essence.

There are certain resemblances between this pattern of spiritual life and that of the Christian saint; but there are also profound differences, resulting from wide divergences of thought about God and the world's relations with him.

Christianity teaches in the first place that God is holy: he is not part of the world. The external world is not an illusion, men and things are real, but they are God's handiwork and he created them at his will. Men depend on God but he does not depend on them: he transcends them. God calls them to be united with him, and that in love, but in this union they still keep their individuality, just as the love of the Father and the Son in the Blessed Trinity does not do away with their personality.

It was not because of any supposition that the world is made up of unrealities that Antony or Simeon Stylites withdrew from it, but because it has been perverted by sin. By uniting their hardships with Christ's sufferings the athletes of penance hoped to contribute to the ransom that he paid; when they pursued the Devil to his lair they were thinking about their erring fellows. They made use of penitential methods reminiscent of those of Hindu mystics because they too were striving for self-mastery and such methods are effective; but they knew all the time that God cannot be obtained by any human efforts, however knowledgeable and persevering they may be. God imparts himself to whom he wills, when he wills; he is free; he is holy: but he loves.

Little is known about the mystical experiences of the early saints, but quite a lot is known about those of the great mystics of later times, since St Teresa and St John of the Cross. We know from them that the life of union with God is possible, because they lived it: but it came to them as a supernatural gift. Had they claimed it through their own efforts they would never have received it.

Like their virtue, the mysticism of the holy men of India is a fine thing; but it is shot through with pantheism and does not emerge from the natural realm. It is one of the peaks that man can attain without knowing the revelation and the redemption of Jesus Christ.

By looking at the lives of saints we have been able to verify experimentally what the Bible teaches us about man's power-lessness to sanctify himself by his own efforts, and that never-theless he is called and enabled to share in the holiness of Christ. And the comparison we have attempted with other high forms of religious life helps us to clarify the significance of this teaching and to appreciate its message of grace more adequately.

# PART TWO

# THE VENERATION OF THE SAINTS

# CHAPTER IV

# ORIGIN AND DEVELOPMENT

Veneration (*cultus*) of saints has a considerable part in the life of the Catholic Church. The importance given to these holy people sometimes causes surprise and provokes questions. Isn't it a sort of regression to paganism? These people gave their whole life to God, their only love, and would they not be the first to protest against this giving of religious veneration to human beings? Is it not a deforming of the pure word of the Gospel? Were not Protestants right to condemn and reject it? Such questions are worth asking, and they must be seriously considered.

The origin of the veneration of saints has first to be sought in the Church's history, and its development followed down to the forms it takes today. We can then ask ourselves what religious value it has, and what the Church owes to the saints whom she reveres and to whom she prays.

## THE CULTUS OF MARTYRS

The veneration of saints in the Christian Church began with the honour paid to her martyrs.

It cannot be questioned that the earliest Christians had a religious reverence for the Apostles and for the Virgin Mary. And it is probable that, when those who had lived in intimacy with their divine Master and had handed on the faith to them were dead, the faithful addressed prayers to them privately. But a public *cultus* of saints appears only in the second century, in connection with the death and burial of martyrs.

It is from a very valuable and striking document of the year 155 that we learn how the public veneration of martyrs began in local Churches. An aged man named Polycarp, eighty-six years old, a disciple of the apostle St John, and bishop of the Christians at Smyrna, had been done to death in the stadium by order of the Roman proconsul. The Smyrniot Christians sent an account of his passion to a church some distance away, which had asked for it. In it we read that, after the martyrdom, a certain Niketas asked the governor not to give up Polycarp's body to his friends, "Lest," he said, "they leave the man who was crucified and begin to worship this man". The writer goes on:

> He was induced to say this by the Jews, who were watching for us to take the body from the fire. They do not know that we can never either forsake Christ, who suffered for the salvation of those who are being saved throughout the world—the innocent One for the guilty—or worship anybody else. We worship him as Son of God; but we love the martyrs as followers and imitators of the Lord, and they deserve that we should, because of their wholehearted attachment to their sovereign and teacher. May we too be of their company and equally faithful.
>
> So when the centurion saw the attitude of the Jews, he put the body back on the pyre and burnt it, according to custom. Then at last we were able to take up the bones—more precious than precious stones and finer than gold—and put them in a fitting place. There the Lord will enable us to meet together in joy and gladness to celebrate the day whereon Polycarp was born through martyrdom; this we shall do in memory of those who have fought the good fight and as training and preparation for contests to come.

Notice, in passing, the ironical words of Niketas, himself a Jew, which represent the objection brought against *cultus* of the saints from that day to this: the argument that veneration of a human being may take the place of worship of the one and only Saviour, Jesus Christ. The answer of the writer of the letter is to the point. It is clear that Christians took the danger into account from the beginning; but they decided that it was not a sufficient reason for depriving themselves of a stimulus to love of Christ: the stimulus to be found in the recollection and celebration of the example given by those who loved him enough to die in torment for him.[1]

## BEFORE MARTYRDOM

The admiration for martyrs that is so clear in the letter from Smyrna about St Polycarp was equally lively in other communities of that era. All second- and third-century Christian writings declare that there is no more enviable lot than to die for Christ. Re-read the letter of St Ignatius and the Passion of St Perpetua, or the letter from the Christians of Lyons and Vienne which we might have quoted—it is as fine as either.[2] There is the same enthusiasm, the same wondering reverence for the bravery of the old bishop Pothinus, the deacon Sanctus and the young slave-girl Blandina. They are the heroes and heroines of the new people. Everybody dreams of dying like them, even those who are frightened of suffering: they become bold when they see how Christ comes to sustain by his presence those who are as weak as themselves.

There is anguish in a church when persecution falls on it; but it is felt as a great honour too. Will those who have been arrested stand up to the threat of torture? What heavenly joy, what pride, there is everywhere when they are questioned and stand firm in the faith, when they *confess*, that is, acknowledge their name of Christian before the judge! Now they have

[1] There is a translation of the Martyrdom of Polycarp in the Ancient Christian Writers series, Vol. VI (London, 1957, Westminster, Md., 1948).
[2] For texts of and excerpts from records of martyrdom in all ages, see D. Attwater, *Martyrs* (London and New York, 1958).

to be given as much help as prison-regulations will allow: material help, testimonies of respect and admiration, spiritual encouragement from the leaders of the church of which they are now the champions. It is they who represent it before the world and before God: may they persevere to the end, may these confessors become martyrs! The brethren, scattered among the crowd, are breathless with dread and admiration, lingering there to the last, while there is any life left in those tormented bodies, awaiting the final witness when death shall set them free and take these heroes to Christ for ever.

Later the brethren come with every sign of religious reverence to venerate the bodies of the dead, which have borne so much and will, thanks to those sufferings, rise again in glory with Christ. No wonder that the people of Smyrna called them "more precious than precious stones and finer than gold".

## THE TOMB AND THE ANNIVERSARY

The Greco-Roman world in which new-born Christianity was rooted had the greatest respect for the burial-places of the dead. A grave was a sacred and inviolable place. When the body of a dead man had been buried, the law regarded any violation of his tomb as a crime, no matter what the man's character or religion had been. It was not lawful to move a body from one grave to another; and Roman roads were sometimes taken out of their course to avoid disturbing an old cemetery.

The early Christians drew much advantage from this legislation. When the bodies of martyrs were not withheld from them after death, they could bury them and look after the graves with every security. They could also meet together at these burying-places for commemorative rites, which were customary among the heathen as well. The most important of these occasions was the anniversary. But whereas the heathen every year celebrated the anniversary of birth, Christians celebrated that of burial, the *depositio*. Polycarp's disciples give as the reason for this choice of date that the martyr's death is his birthday into the life of blessedness.

The family that gathered round the grave on the anniversary day was no longer confined to relatives: it was the whole Christian family, the whole local Church, for which the grave was a family grave. They were responsible for it. Ordinarily, it did not stand alone; in the big cemeteries it was one tomb among many, but the faithful knew where it was and around it they met for the yearly celebration. There was nothing funereal about this; it was a happy occasion. During the eucharistic Sacrifice, the central act of the feast, the martyr was named. They did not pray *for* him, but in his honour. And the whole was often concluded by a meal in common, of which again the note does not seem to have been sad.

At times of persecution these anniversaries had necessarily to be observed with discretion. But when religious peace allowed more open solemnity there were often considerable crowds, similar to modern pilgrimages. It was to accommodate these, and to add impressiveness to the rites, that basilicas came to be built over the sacred tombs.

## THE FIRST MARTYROLOGIES

Every church had a calendar in which was recorded the anniversary day of each of its martyrs and the place where the faithful had to meet. At Rome, where cemeteries were numerous all round the city, it was called the *Depositio martyrum* and it names the catacomb wherein each anniversary was celebrated. For example:

January 20th: [anniversary] of Fabian [at the cemetery] of Callistus; and of Sebastian, at the Catacombs.
January 21st: [anniversary] of Agnes, on the Mentana road.

August 6th: [anniversary] of Sixtus [at the cemetery] of Callistus; and [at that] of Praetextatus, of Agapitus and Felicissimus.

August 10th: [anniversary] of Lawrence, on the Tivoli road.

Originally these calendars were concerned solely with local martyrs, but soon they began to include the names of some venerated in other churches. The Roman *Depositio martyrum* proves that the Church there in the fourth century kept the anniversaries of Perpetua and Felicity and of Cyprian, all of whom were martyred and buried in Africa. It was at this time, too, that the names of the Apostles and St Stephen began to be inserted among those of more recent martyrs; and very soon after, at the end of the fourth or beginning of the fifth century, a feast of our Lady appeared in some churches, under the name of Commemoration of the holy Mary.

Thus we see the veneration of the saints attain its fullness. It had begun with each local Church honouring the martyrs whose tombs it had and cared for; now it includes saints of the whole Church, universal in place and time.

## INVOCATION OF MARTYRS

The giving of public reverence to a martyr does not necessarily mean that prayers are addressed *to* him: the dead can be honoured without praying to and invoking them. However, it is known that the Christians of the first centuries freely invoked, not only the martyrs, but those, especially relatives, who had died in peace. There are hundreds of memorial inscriptions in the catacombs bearing the name of the person buried there and asking his or her prayers. Here are translations of a few:

[Here lies] the faithful Gentian in peace, who lived 21 years, 8 months and 16 days. Intercede for us in your prayers, for we know you are in Christ.

Pray for your parents, Matronata Matrona, who lived 1 year and 52 days.

Sabbatius, kind soul, pray and intercede for your brothers and companions.

Mercury set up [this inscription] to his most worthy wife Justa, who lived with me for 14 years and had 7 children, of whom 2 survive. Pray, [Justa,] pray for them.[1]

There is nothing surprising about such invocations; they are a quite natural consequence of belief in the soul's immortality and in the fellowship of souls in Christ. The soul's life after death is not a diminished life, a shadowy reflection of life on earth: it is the flowering in God of all that was good in it; and all souls living in Christ are united as members of a single body. What more natural then that those who have victoriously finished their earthly course should be concerned for those who are still in the battle? They go on praying for those dear to them, as they prayed when on earth; and in God's light their prayer is more effective than ever. At the death of Paula, the widow whom he had directed in the ascetic way, St Jerome exclaimed: "Good-bye, Paula! This old man reveres you: sustain him by your prayers during his closing years. May your faith and your good works unite you with Christ; in his presence you will the more easily obtain what you ask."

These invocations were addressed to departed faithful whose lives had not been crowned by martyrdom. Martyrs could be turned to still more confidently, since their place in Heaven and Christ's predilection for them were certain. But it was then no longer the dead man's family alone that asked his prayers: he was a specially glorious member of his Church and all his Church invoked him. St Ambrose wrote: "They, who have washed away their sins (if they had any) in their own blood, can ask grace for our sins; they are God's martyrs and our leaders, who testify to our life and what we do. We need not blush to

[1] For the texts of these and other inscriptions, and the whole subject, see H. Delehaye, *Les origines du culte des martyrs* (Bruxelles, 1933).

take them as intercessors in our weakness; they too knew the body's weaknesses, even as they overcame them."

And St Augustine, who often preached at the anniversaries of martyrs, sets out the Church's teaching clearly when he distinguishes sharply between the martyrs and the commonalty of faithful. "The martyrs are perfected in righteousness", he says, "and they earned perfection through their martyrdom. For them the Church does not pray: for the other departed faithful she prays, but not for martyrs. They have gone out of this world so perfected that instead of being our clients they are our advocates."

It is good to know that the invocation of saints and belief in their power to intercede for us are as old as the Church herself. These things are among the most authentic elements of Christian revelation.

## FROM MARTYRS TO CONFESSORS

Many of those who confessed Christ at the peril of their lives were not afterwards put to death: they were sentenced to penal labour in distant quarries or died naturally in prison. These were looked on as martyrs equally with those who shed their blood. Others there were who were set at liberty, especially upon a change in imperial policy. These and other survivors were not martyrs but *confessors*, and they took a high place in their church. At divine worship, for instance, they ranked with priests. St Cyprian, at Carthage, directed that the date of death of confessors should be carefully recorded, so that their anniversaries could be observed.

Fervent Christians whom God did not call to witness by blood had often to be consoled with the assurance that, in God's eyes, a desire for martyrdom is equivalent to martyrdom, when only its circumstances are wanting. In these terms Cyprian comforted the faithful who, during an epidemic, would rather have died at the hands of the executioner than simply of the plague.

St Jerome and St John Chrysostom declare that ordinary Christian life is a kind of daily martyrdom, if it be lived lovingly and all its renunciations taken as a permanent self-offering. And St Athanasius says in his Life of St Antony that, when Antony returned to the wilderness after risking his life to help the persecuted faithful at Alexandria, he had to battle more fiercely with evil spirits in his hermitage than with any judge in a court.

## ASCETICS

Such considerations as these became the more timely as persecution lessened and the periods of religious peace lengthened. The ascetics began to succeed the martyrs as heroes of the faith. The attention and admiration of the faithful, formerly directed to those who were tortured or thrown to wild beasts, was given to those who lived in a state of constant austerity. St Antony went further and further into the desert as much to escape the attentions of his admirers as to bring the Evil One to battle; and it has been wittily said of St Simeon that, "despairing of escaping the world horizontally, he tried to escape it vertically".

The burial of these penitential athletes was carried out as solemnly as the *depositio* of a martyr, and their names, as confessors, were entered side by side with those of martyrs in the martyrologies. St Antony died in the year 356, and his feast was being celebrated in the lifetime of St Hilarion, who died in 372; and there is proof that the feast of Hilarion himself was observed immediately after his death.

## BISHOPS

Among other names that were soon added to martyrologies were those of certain bishops: men who were known for their influential activity and their writings, such as St Ambrose at

Milan, or for their austere life and apostolic works, such as St Martin of Tours. And their *cultus* spread far beyond the limits of their own Church.

Other bishops who had been neither martyrs nor ascetics had feasts in their own dioceses simply because it was the custom to observe the anniversary of their burial. In the Roman Church there were two distinct lists: the *Depositio martyrum*, which has been mentioned, and a similar *Depositio episcoporum*, which recorded the date and place for the celebration of the anniversary of deceased bishops. Thus:

> December 26th: [anniversary] of Dionysius [at the cemetery] of Callistus.
> December 29th: [anniversary] of Felix [at the cemetery] of Callistus.
> December 31st: [anniversary] of Silvester [at the cemetery] of Priscilla.

Later on the two lists were combined into one. In some Churches, of which Carthage was one, it looks as if this fusion was made from the first. We have something like it still, when diocesan calendars include the dates of the anniversaries of previous bishops.

But this does not mean that at the beginning there was any confusion of martyrs, who were invoked, with simple bishops, who were prayed for. This is proved by the fact that at Rome martyred bishops were named in the *Depositio martyrum* and not in the *Depositio episcoporum*. But it is known that there was a *cultus* of St Silvester (d. 335; bishop, not a martyr) in Rome before the end of the fifth century; and, as we have just seen, he figured in the *Depositio episcoporum*, on December 31st.

It was difficult for transferences from one classification to another to come about spontaneously so long as the memories of their martyrs and their bishops were fresh in the minds of the faithful. But as these memories became blurred, and names of confessors were multiplied in the martyrologies, it was only natural that the honours given to ascetics should also be accorded to bishops. So they in their turn became confessors. It is worth noticing that Sidonius Apollinaris, the biographer of St Martin of Tours, whom he had known, calls him "bishop and confessor" (Letter 4, 18), the title under which the Church still venerates him.

St Martin was venerated as a saint at once after his death in 397, but he was an exception. Diocesan episcopal lists include a large number of very early bishops decorated with the title of Saint; but it is probable that many of them acquired it only through the passage of time, by a fusing of the two lists of which martyrologies were originally composed.

# CHAPTER V

# CANONIZATION

The question "What is a saint?" could in one sense be answered in this way: "A saint is a person, now dead, whom the Church allows to be publicly venerated". And when we look at the actual regulations governing the procedure of canonization we see that nowadays this permission is not given lightly. The procedure has not always been so rigorous, as indeed our account of the origins of the *cultus* of saints would lead one to expect. Let us then add a brief account of the successive forms that the approval of *cultus* has taken.

## THE EARLIER CENTURIES

So far as martyrs are concerned, no procedure was necessary. The faithful had been present at the martyr's trial and execution, and could see for themselves that he had stoutly confessed Christ and had been put to death for it. His bodily remains had been recovered and religiously entombed. The date and place of burial were entered on the official record of the local church, inscribed in the canon: this was *canonization*.[1]

Some cases were not so simple. It sometimes happened that, together with orthodox Catholics, heretics and schismatics, such as Marcionites or Donatists, were put to death. There does

[1] The word *canon* has a number of meanings, all deriving ultimately from the original one: a reed or tube. A reed or tube could be used to measure with, as a pattern or rule, and it is this sense that gives us *canon* of the Mass, *canon* law, and so on. In our context, the canon is an official list of saints.

not seem to have been any hesitation about these: it was at once admitted that those who died outside the Church could not be counted among her martyrs. On the other hand, indulgence was shown to those who were martyred after having forsaken her communion and then returned to it. The most famous case is that of St Hippolytus.

Hippolytus was a Roman priest, who was very put out when the deacon Callistus was elected to the chair of St Peter in 217: he had a poor opinion of Callistus and was critical of some of his theological opinions. Hippolytus became head of a schismatic party, and was an antipope for some fifteen years. The second successor of St Callistus was St Pontian, who was arrested in 235, during the persecution under Maximinus. Hippolytus was arrested at the same time, and pope and antipope were together deported to the island of Sardinia. Pontian, thinking that he would never see Rome again, resigned the papal see, and it is probable that Hippolytus withdrew his pretensions at the same time; he told his followers to return to the fold, for the schism was then at an end. Both men died in exile, and when their bodies were brought back to Rome they were both regarded as martyrs. Pontian was buried with his predecessors in the cemetery of Callistus, and Hippolytus in the cemetery on the Via Tiburtina, which henceforth was known by his name and became a much frequented place of pilgrimage.

In such an important case as this, decisions could not have been taken without the bishop's approval, and it was the same when it was a question of officially recognizing as martyrs those confessors who died at the mines and quarries or in prison. It is known that African bishops had often to intervene to put a stop to the veneration of bogus martyrs—criminals who had been killed in a brawl with unbelievers, or fanatics who had deliberately provoked the authorities without just cause.

In most cases a bishop signified his approval simply by associating himself with the spontaneous recognition by his flock; occasionally he had to oppose it. It may be said, then, that it was the bishop who approved a *cultus* in the Church that he shepherded.

## THE LATER EMPIRE AND MIDDLE AGES

In the year 386 the bishop St Ambrose built a basilica in Milan, but it lacked the shrine of a martyr, such as the Roman basilicas had been built over and which contributed so much to their sacredness. Ambrose then had, he wrote to his sister (Letter 22), not a revelation but a kind of intuition. In accordance therewith, he dug beneath another church and there found the bodies of two very tall men, "like those of olden time", with all bones intact and a lot of blood.

We are not told how he knew that these were the bodies of martyrs, and of Gervase and Protase in particular. However, they were solemnly transferred to the new basilica (which later bore the name of St Ambrose, and still does); and during the procession a blind man received his sight. Thus was the bishop's intuition confirmed and the *cultus* of the two martyrs approved. This is one of the first times that the veneration of a saint was allowed without reference to what had till then been the sole criterion: the testimony of contemporaries to death and burial, handed on from age to age by an unbroken tradition.

Such findings of relics became rather frequent during the centuries that followed, and the criterion of authenticity was always the same: visions through which the relics were identified, and miracles that took place through contact with them. Here, for instance, is the origin of the *cultus* of St Benignus at Dijon, as related by St Gregory of Tours in his *In gloria martyrum* (late sixteenth century).

At the beginning of that century Gregory's great-grandfather, also called Gregory, who was bishop of Langres, lived at Dijon. There was a big sarcophagus there, which the bishop and everybody else took to be that of a heathen man. People came in from the country, however, to pray at this tomb, and their requests were promptly granted. One day a man brought a lighted candle as a thank-offering, which a child tried to snatch; but at that very moment a big snake curled round the candle. This happened several times, and the people got so excited that the bishop forbade them to pray there. But then he was told in a vision that it was really a martyr, named Benignus, who was buried in the tomb. "What are you doing?" the martyr asked. "You not only despise me, but you even drive away those who would honour me. Stop·this, please, and build a shelter for my grave at once." Other miracles accompanied the construction of the chapel, over which a basilica was soon built. Some years later travellers from Italy brought a written account of the martyrdom of Benignus to Gregory of Langres.

Thus Gregory of Tours. The Passion of St Benignus referred to is in fact nothing but a fiction, crammed with anachronisms; but it had great popularity in the Carolingian era and carried the veneration of the alleged martyr throughout Burgundy and beyond.

This case is, unhappily, by no means an isolated one. During the Merovingian and following centuries there can be found hundreds of examples of the *cultus* of saints being recognized on equally flimsy grounds. And many of the saints concerned are still very popular.

## SANCTION BY ROME

It appears that Rome did not at first lay claim to a control of canonizations. The first recourses to the Holy See for approval of the enshrinement (*elevatio*) of the relics of a bishop or abbot date from around the year 1000. The oldest that we know was in 993, when a bishop of Augsburg, during a synod presided over by Pope John XV, asked permission to read to the assembly an account of the life and miracles of his predecessor, Ulric. This done, the pope declared, with the unanimous agreement of those present, that it was right and proper to venerate the memory of this holy bishop. That was, as yet in very summary form, the first recorded *process* of canonization.

Sanction by Rome necessarily gave increased dignity to an enshrinement of relics in the diocese of the saint concerned, and especially did it give neighbouring dioceses an assurance of the genuineness of the new saint and the reality of his merits. The imaginative fancies that were too often at work in local canonizations had, understandably enough, brought them into some disrepute.

It was Pope Alexander III (1159-81), the defender of the Church's rights against Frederick Barbarossa and Henry II of England, who decided that in future causes of canonization should be reserved to the Holy See, and that no one should have the right to give a public *cultus* to any man, "however many miracles he may have done", without authority from the Roman Church.[1]

## URBAN VIII'S LEGISLATION

From the twelfth century onwards the procedure in causes of canonization at Rome was made increasingly explicit until, in 1634, Pope Urban VIII laid down the broad lines of the rules for approval of *cultus* as they are today.

The thousands of canonizations that had taken place previously were not called in question: local cults were given the benefit of a prescription of one hundred years, and the pope gave global permissive approval to all canonizations of before 1534. But henceforward the fact that a spontaneous public *cultus* had been given to a deceased person was no longer to be regarded as a first step towards canonization: on the contrary, it was to be regarded as an obstacle in its way. Until Rome has declared somebody to be Blessed, it is forbidden to set up images showing him or her with a halo or other indications of sanctity; or to publish writings about his holiness,

[1] On this subject see E. W. Kemp, *Canonization and Authority in the Western Church* (Oxford, 1948).

revelations, miracles or martyrdom unaccompanied by a declaration that the writer has no intention of anticipating the judgements of the Holy See on these matters.

The decrees of Urban VIII were discussed in a classic work, published in 1734–8, by Cardinal Prosper Lambertini, who completed them when he became pope as Benedict XIV. They reached their definitive formulation in the Code of Canon Law of 1917.

## BEATIFICATION

The law provides for two stages in canonization. After the first the servant of God is declared *Beatus*, Blessed. For centuries this term was equivalent to *Sanctus*, Saint; but it is now used to designate any deceased person whom the Holy See allows to be publicly venerated in a particular place or by a particular religious order or congregation. This authorization is only provisional, it could be revoked for good reason, and veneration of the *Beatus* is not incumbent on the Church at large. Nevertheless the title is not bestowed until after minute inquiries and considered decisions: the bishop of the place concerned has to collect all the writings of the servant of God, to take evidence from witnesses about his life and miracles, and to make sure that there has been no public *cultus* by anticipation.

The pertinent documents are then forwarded to Rome, where they are examined by the Congregation of Rites. The study of the candidate's writings alone often involves a very great deal of work. If the cardinals' opinion is favourable, the pope declares the cause to be introduced. The process properly so called then takes place, before judges appointed by the prefect of the Congregation of Rites: this goes on first in the diocese concerned, where inquiry is made into the candidate's life and where his relics are identified; then at Rome, where judgement is made on the heroism of his virtue or the reality of his martyrdom. When either of these is proved, the pope declares that the servant of God may be styled Venerable.

If it be not a matter of martyrdom, at least two miracles must be proved, with the help of physicians or other experts. On their being accepted, the pope declares that beatification may be proceeded with, and the decree is published in due course.

If it were discovered that public veneration had been accorded at any time before beatification, the cause would be suspended; it then could not be taken up again until after a period of time whose length would be laid down by authority.

## CANONIZATION

Beatification is a provisional measure. The pope can complete, confirm and extend it by canonization.

Canonization is a definitive act, and one that formally and irrevocably involves the Church's teaching authority. Theologians are almost unanimously of the opinion that it is a judgement involving papal infallibility.

To go on to canonization a process must be carried through analogous to that for beatification, but it is principally concerned with the proof of two more miracles wrought through the intercession of the *Beatus* since he was beatified.[1] It concludes with a rite of special solemnity in St Peter's basilica, in the course of which the pope pronounces the final judgement: "To the honour of the holy and undivided Trinity. . . . We decree and define that the blessed N . . . is a saint, and We enter his name in the roll of saints, ordering that his memory be religiously venerated every year by the Church throughout the world . . .".

The person canonized is thenceforth referred to by the title Saint (*sanctus*, holy), before his first name: Saint John Fisher, Saint Pius X.[2]

[1] In 1935 St John Fisher and St Thomas More were canonized with dispensation from proof of miracles. It was the first example of this since the legislation of Urban VIII. [*Trans.*]

[2] In the liturgical prayers (collects, etc.) of the Western Church a saint is usually referred to as "the blessed N . . .", "the blessed martyr N . . .", etc. There is a useful short account of current practice in a C.T.S. pamphlet, *The Canonization of Saints*, by Mgr P. E. Hallett. [*Trans.*]

## SAINT N ...

Apostles and martyrs began to be invoked as Saint So-and-so from the fifth century. Before that they were addressed and referred to more casually, without any title. When in the third century the faithful at Rome had prayed to the apostles Peter and Paul in the catacombs and then refreshed themselves in their honour, they scratched on the walls of the dining-room: "Paul and Peter pray for Victor", "Paul and Peter, be mindful of Sozomen", "Peter and Paul, pray for Leonitus", and so on. The same brevity is found in funeral inscriptions and on early paintings, where the martyr's name stands beside his image.

On the other hand, the word "holy" was often used as a term of respect for anyone whose office had a sacred character, the emperor, for instance, or a bishop. It was a polite convention, which had no reference to the personal character of the man to whom it was applied. When he wrote to the emperor Gratian, St Ambrose did not hesitate to address him as "Sancte imperator". It was normal and usual practice to refer to a deceased bishop as, e.g., "Bishop Aurelian of holy memory", and during his lifetime to speak to him with the honorific "Your Holiness". Later on other forms became fashionable; till lately, bishops in France were "Grandeur", archbishops in England are still "Grace": but the bishop of Rome, the pope, remains "Holiness".

People adopted the usage of adding Saint to a martyr's name both in order to honour an outstanding person of sacred character and to recognize the greatness of his or her virtues. We have the same intentions today when we reserve the same title to those whom the chief bishop of the holy people of God offers to us as models, allowing us publicly to venerate them because he knows that they are living in God.

C H A P T E R  V I

# THE ROMAN

# MARTYROLOGY

The Roman Martyrology is an official liturgical book, forming a catalogue of saints recognized by the Catholic Church. They are arranged according to the days of the year on which their annual feast-days occur, with a note of the place where their *cultus* originated. Most of the entries have also a few lines of explanation, stating what the saint was and did, and how he or she died. Here, by way of example, are the entries for February 1st, which is the feast-day of St Ignatius of Antioch in the general calendar of the Western Church, the first saint of whom an account is given in Chapter II above.

[The feast] of St Ignatius, bishop of Antioch and martyr, who fulfilled a glorious witness on December 20 [on which date a longer notice is accorded him].

At Smyrna, of St Pionius, priest and martyr, who wrote vindications of the Christian faith. After confinement in a vile prison, where by his earnest words he encouraged many of the brethren to undergo martyrdom and himself endured many torments, he was pierced with nails and laid upon a burning pyre; and thus he reached a blessed end for Christ. Fifteen others suffered with him.

At Ravenna, of St Severus, bishop, whose election was indicated by a dove because of his outstanding merits.

At the town of Trois-Châteaux in France, of St Paul, bishop, whose life was distinguished for virtue and his holy death approved by miracles.

At Kildare in Ireland, of St Brigid, virgin, who in proof of her maidenhood touched the wood of an altar which at once became green.

At Castelfiorentino in Tuscany, of the blessed Verdiana, virgin, a recluse of the Vallombrosan Order.

There are similar entries for every day of the year. It is directed that, in churches wherein the Divine Office is celebrated in choir, the Martyrology shall be publicly read in Latin at the early morning office of Prime. Priests who recite the Breviary privately are not bound to read the Martyrology, but they are encouraged to do so; in many seminaries and religious communities it is read in public after the midday meal.

Like most liturgical books, the Roman Martyrology is the product of a very ancient tradition; and it is desirable to know its history in order to appreciate what the Church wants us to learn when she encourages us to read it.

## ORIGINS

We have seen in Chapter IV how the first martyrologies were compiled in local Churches, and that various local lists were fused together to make general martyrologies. So it came about that in Rome of the fifth century a list took shape of the saints of Italy, Africa and the East: this became associated with the name of St Jerome, and so is generally called the Hieronymian Martyrology. Like the *Depositio martyrum* which it incorporated, it simply gave, according to the days of the year, the name and date of burial of each saint, and the place of burial, or at any rate the place of origin of the anniversary.

For centuries the Hieronymian Martyrology was recopied many times by scribes in various countries, and each time with additions, corrections and accidental mistakes. It is one of the manuscript documents whose primitive form is the most difficult to restore; but it is the one that became the kernel of the Roman Martyrology.

In the eighth century that careful English scholar St Bede, called the Venerable, had the idea of adding to each saint's name a short notice giving some particulars of his life and death, so far as they could be ascertained. Bede got his information from the "acts" of the martyrs and from the writings of historians and fathers of the Church. His enterprise was the origin of the brief notes that ordinarily accompany each entry in the Roman Martyrology today.

Bede kept the grouping of saints according to the day of burial or the translation of their relics, and so he had all but half the days of the year without any entries. In the following century three authors in succession set themselves to complete Bede's work, with elements of very unequal value.

The first was Florus, a deacon of Lyons in the year 800, who filled 52 of the 181 days left blank by Bede. The rest were filled fifty years later by another man from Lyons, Ado; he became archbishop of Vienne, but he did not have the scholarly competence and professional conscientiousness of his predecessors. He did not scruple to invent when he had no documents to use, not worrying about misleading those who would trust him in ages to come. One of these was Usuard, a monk of the abbey of Saint-Germain-des-Près before the end of the ninth century; he was commissioned by Charles the Bald to compile a calendar that should be in some sort official, so as "to restore a degree of concord to the solemnities of the saints".

This was the Martyrology of Usuard, which was the most popular for the rest of the Middle Ages. Inevitably it was touched up and added to from time to time. When the printing of liturgical books began in the fifteenth century, it was used as the basis of the earliest editions of the work published under the title of Martyrology of the Holy Roman Church.

## OFFICIAL EDITIONS

Towards the end of the sixteenth century, Pope Gregory XIII, to whose reform the world owes the annual calendar that it uses today, determined to complete this reform by the publication of an official edition of the Martyrology. He appointed a commission for the work, whose leading spirit was the learned Oratorian, Cesare Baronius, who was made cardinal a few years later. The first complete edition appeared in 1584.

Baronius was an erudite and conscientious scholar. His aim was not to compile a new martyrology, but so far as possible to restore its most ancient forms, freed from more recent disfigurements. In effect he settled for the Martyrology of Usuard, which he completed from the acts of martyrs, patristic writings, the Greek liturgical books, and so forth. The result is a composite work, the value of whose contents from the historical point of view is very unequal, depending on the sources from which they were derived. When the names given have been faithfully recopied from age to age since the original list of each Church was drawn up, we are confronted by ancient and most valuable testimony. When a notice is simply a summary of one of the numerous passions and legends composed during the Middle Ages, its worth is that of the document from which it is drawn—and often that is very little.

To give a notion of the complexity of the Roman Martyrology, consider the sources of the entries for February 1st, as set out above.

The Hieronymian Martyrology does not mention *St Ignatius of Antioch*. Bede put him on December 17th. Ado entered him on February 1st, and wrote a notice from which the present one on December 20th is taken. Florus was the first to name *St Pionius*. The notice was drawn up by Usuard, from an account of solid value. But the attribution of fifteen companions to him is due to confusion with another Pionius. *St Severus of Ravenna* figures in Hieronymian manuscripts. *St Paul of Trois-Châteaux* was inserted by Florus. *St Brigid*, who died *c.* 525, appears in several Hieronymian manuscripts; the legend was added by Ado. *Bd Verdiana* was beatified by Pope Clement VII in 1533, and her name was entered in the Martyrology in 1673.[1]

There have been many re-editions of the Roman Martyrology of Baronius; the current one is dated 1956. Small corrections of detail have been made each time, and saints canonized since the previous edition are added to the days of their feasts.

The Church's infallibility extends to canonizations that have taken place since 1534 and to no others. She simply authorizes the veneration of other saints whose names figure in the Martyrology, being those that had a prescription of a hundred years or more; this is a disciplinary provision, which does not cover, from the point of view of doctrine, any errors into which the authors of the old martyrologies may have fallen. The Church encourages learned men to pursue their studies in this diverse and complex mass of material, in order that they may sort out what is authentic from what is doubtful or mistaken. We shall see that willing workers in this field are not lacking.[2]

## LOCAL MARTYROLOGIES

There are many saints whose *cultus* is authorized by the Church but who are not named in the Roman Martyrology. They mostly figure in diocesan martyrologies or in those of religious orders, and their public veneration was allowed to continue by Urban VIII's general approbation. These local martyrologies form a sort of supplement to the Roman Martyrology for each diocese and order. There are, accordingly, many baptismal names that are the names of recognized saints, even though they are not mentioned in the Roman Martyrology itself.[3]

[1] Very few *beati* or *beatae* are included in the Roman Martyrology. St Ephrem of Edessa (named by Bede on another date) was assigned to February 1st by Florus, and Baronius followed him, but he has now been transferred to June 18th. [*Trans.*]

[2] There is an English translation of the Roman Martyrology (London, 1937).

[3] There are also, of course, all the official synaxaries and calendars of the Eastern Churches. [*Trans.*]

# CHAPTER VII

# THE RELICS OF THE SAINTS

We have seen that the *cultus* of saints began at their burying-places. Their bodily remains (which is the literal meaning of the word "relics") were treasured as we treasure keepsakes of those we love. They were revered because those bodies had been temples of the Holy Spirit, and were hallowed by martyrdom or penance. They had suffered, so it was right that they should be honoured. They were revered because they would rise again at the end of time, they were so to say the seed of glorified bodies to come.

At different times this veneration took different forms, of unequal religious worth.

## EARLY DISCIPLINE

The Church of Rome long remained faithful to the law which forbade interference with graves. It was the position of a grave that governed the site and plan of basilican churches. Rather than disturb a tomb, enormous jobs of terracing were done, as in the case of St Peter's burial-place at Rome itself.

Near the end of the sixth century an empress at Constantinople asked Pope St Gregory the Great to send her some bones from St Paul's body, for the imperial chapel that was dedicated in that apostle's honour. Gregory refused the sovereign's request: recent happenings had shown how dangerous it was to disturb the sacred remains of the holy apostles and martyrs; when St Lawrence's tomb was accidentally opened, all those who looked at his body, without even venturing to touch it, were dead within ten days. "Your Majesty must know," he wrote, "that it is not the Roman custom to dare to touch the bodies when relics of saints are given away: all that we do is to send a piece of silk or linen that has been laid upon the sacred body. This is put in a coffer of boxwood . . ." (*Registr.*, iv, 30).

Thus it came about that popes sent to their colleagues in the episcopate white scarves, ornamented with small crosses, that had lain for a time on St Peter's tomb. And this was the origin of the *pallium* which the pope still sends to archbishops and a few privileged bishops of the Western Church. The *pallium* is simply a "relic" of St Peter.

## TRANSFERENCE OF RELICS

To refuse to move a dead body was the finest and most fitting way of showing its sacredness; and it was also the best way of ensuring its genuineness. But other Churches were less wise and less scrupulous than that of Rome, and from the middle of the fourth century Churches in the East were not hesitating to transfer, "translate", the bodies of martyrs, or to dismember them in favour of other Churches.

The new capital of the empire, Constantinople, founded after the era of persecution, had had no martyrs and in this respect was at a disadvantage in face of the old Rome. It was decided to import them. The emperors set the example, and the dismemberment of bodies and moving about of relics were soon in full swing. It is true that this had the effect of encouraging and extending *cultus* of the saints throughout the Christian world; but it also had the lamentable result of making the genuineness of saints' relics very difficult to ensure and control, and it opened the door to all sorts of frauds and sacrilegious dealing.

It became impossible to maintain the traditional rule even in Rome. Fifty years after St Gregory's refusal to the empress

Constantina, a number of bodies of saints were removed from suburban cemeteries to within the shelter of the ramparts. In the following century such translations became more numerous, almost general, because of profanations by the Lombards.

## SALE AND THEFT

From this time on many requests for relics reached Rome from churches and monasteries in the West. The trustingness of pilgrims was often taken advantage of by people whose business it was to satisfy their piety, just as later on the "innocence" of crusaders was exploited by Levantine traders.

Theft of relics was a common manifestation of perverted devotion. We are told that about 1030 the monks of St Augustine's abbey at Canterbury acquired the relics of St Mildred by strategy, and carried them off more or less by force from their resting-place at Minster-in-Thanet. In 1177 a canon regular of Bodmin in Cornwall stole St Petroc's relics from the church of his own monastery, escaped oversea to Brittany, and presented them to the abbey of Saint-Méen; it took the intervention of King Henry II to get them back again. The relics of St Faith (Foy) were stolen from Agen in France in 866 by a monk of Conques. He was a trusted guest of the clergy of Agen, when one day he kicked in the side of the shrine and carried the relics off in a sack. An eleventh-century pilgrim to Conques seems to have approved of this performance, in view of the miracles alleged at St Faith's shrine at Conques.

Nor must it be supposed that this sort of mentality came to an end with the Middle Ages, as the following incident shows. On July 4th, 1583, nine months after the funeral, the tomb of St Teresa of Avila was opened. Father Ribera, who was present, describes the state of the body; it was washed and reclothed, but before wrapping it in a shroud "Father Provincial cut off the left hand". The Father Provincial responsible for this gruesome butchery was Father Gracián, and he completes the story himself, with unashamed naïvety: "I wrapped the hand in paper and took it away in a coif; it gave off an oil. . . . I have left it at Avila in a sealed box. . . When I cut off the hand I also cut off a little finger, which I carry on me. . . . When I was captured by the Turks they took it from me, and I redeemed it for about twenty reals and some gold rings."[1]

Mother Teresa of Jesus was very fond of Father Gracián, but she always distrusted his naïvety. As she looked down from Heaven on this mutilation of her wonderfully preserved body, she may well have thought, in her gently roguish way, that she had been right to be mistrustful.

## MODERN DISCIPLINE

In spite of such excesses and abuses in practice (which can be prevented today), the Church approves and encourages the veneration of relics. Canon law lays down exact rules to ensure their authenticity and to regulate their veneration.

The reasons behind this veneration are the same now as in the early ages. Even if divided up, relics remain precious tokens of remembrance, fragments of bodies hallowed by the Holy Spirit, bodies, too, which we know will rise again in glory. Miracles have often been wrought in connection with them.

Because of their sacredness, tiny relics are sealed into the stone table of every altar when the bishop consecrates it. In days gone by the altar was above the tomb itself. Later, when it was question of a confessor, the bones were solemnly taken out of the tomb and "elevated" above the ground: that is, they were put beneath the altar stone in an elaborate reliquary, or high in a shrine behind the altar. Surely the best place for them is still in the altar itself, under the sacrificial stone, for this position most effectively shows forth the significance of those bodies of the saints in the union of their sacrifice with Christ's sacrifice.

[1] M. Auclair, *La vie de sainte Thérèse d'Avila*, pp. 473–4. Eng. trans. *Saint Teresa of Avila*, trans. by K. Pond, with a preface by André Maurois, p. 431 (London and New York, 1953).

CHAPTER VIII

# SAINTS AT WORK IN

# THE CHURCH

Having examined the origin and history of the veneration of saints and its integral place in the Church's life from early times, we may now inquire into its meaning and value for the faithful.

Through the *cultus* rendered to them, the saints in Heaven continue to be an influence in the Church as they were when on earth. The work that they began then they carry on now: death has not made a break. They prayed for their brethren in this life, and they still pray for them in heavenly bliss. Their inspiring effect on their fellows is not lessened when personal contacts are replaced by our pondering the lessons to be learned from their teaching and example.

Accordingly, we will consider what the saints have been and what they still are for Christians who call upon them, without separating their activity on earth from its continuation in Heaven.

## *WITNESSES*

The first saints, those who gave their lives for Christ, were called martyrs, that is, witnesses, and in a real sense that name can be applied to all other saints too. For they also bear witness: by their lives, as martyrs by their deaths, they testify, "confess", to the continuing presence of Christ in his Church.

The Church is called holy because she continues Christ's sanctifying work throughout the ages. It is he acting in her who hallows the newly baptized, it is he who fosters and increases this holiness through the sacraments that the Church ministers. But this activity of Christ is nearly always hidden and unseen: we know it by faith and not with our eyes, because the general run of baptized and practising Christians do not at the first glance seem morally any better than the general run of other people. "The kingdom of heaven is like leaven, that a woman has taken and buried away in three measures of meal, enough to leaven the whole batch" (Matt. 13. 33). Unhappily, the human dough is very solid and the action of the yeast is slow.

But, thank God, there are those in whom the Holy Spirit can be seen to be working, in the souls of the saints. The admiration that they arouse in life and the veneration given them after death show how great are people's joy and thankfulness at what they have seen. What they acclaim is what they, more or less consciously, desire themselves to be; and their spontaneous admiration and gratitude prove that in them too the Holy Spirit's working has not been in vain, even though hidden. They are so glad at last to recognize an achievement such as they have sought, and sought with suffering. They knew all along that the grace by which they lived was strong enough to produce far better images of Christ than the poor sketches that they were themselves. It is not surprising that they should at once be carried away and inspired by a living example of the ever-active presence of the sanctifying Spirit. Whenever a saint arises, he is the point of departure for a renewal of fervour among Christian people.

Nor is this fervour solely a consequence of example. Above all does the saint give confidence to those in whom hope has been no more than dormant. Because of the saint they again become conscious of their own calling to holiness, and they realize that they too are capable of all things, "thanks to the strength that God gives me" (Phil. 4. 13).

## IN TIME OF NEED

A history of the Church could be written in terms of the saints who have marked her course. That course is already a long one. The Church has gone through many crises, each of which has threatened her continued growth. In every age the Holy Spirit who is her life has raised up saints who have understood the needs of their time, and whose wonderful foresight has cleared a way to improvement and security amid thronging difficulties.

The martyrs enabled the Christian faith to triumph in the pagan Roman empire. That empire was not hostile to new religions. It would have gladly welcomed the new god from Palestine among its other gods, just as it had welcomed Cybele and Mithras. Christ's religion would have been assimilated to the other mystery-religions; it would have flourished with them for a time, and then would have died with them. But Christians had intransigently to maintain that there is no god but God, no lord but Jesus Christ: and it is precisely for having maintained that, for refusing to offer a pinch of incense to some other deity, that the martyrs died.

Eventually the emperor Constantine was converted to Christianity and it was no longer dangerous to belong to the Church; people were baptized right and left, though manners and customs were still pagan. Thereupon ascetics took the place of martyrs to show that Christ and the world cannot be worshipped together and that there is no salvation otherwise than through his cross.

When the empire was swamped by the barbarians, the invaders found bishops in the cities, great men who, for all they were unarmed, had their way by force of quiet courage and the nobility of their attitude.

In due course the successors of these bishops were corrupted by feudal anarchy, and the episcopate became a valuable apanage of baronial families: then it was the monastic saints who saved spiritual things. During the dark days of the tenth century, when the papacy itself was enslaved, the monastery of Cluny was preparing reform and renewal in the Western Church.

Three centuries later communal enfranchisement was paving the way for the rise of a new power, that of money: the knights of voluntary poverty, St Francis, St Dominic and their followers, were there, seeking to turn men from the service of mammon.

Torn though she was by the Protestant Reformation, the Church was able to bring about her own internal reform among the peoples that remained faithful to her. This was not due solely to measures taken at the Council of Trent: it was also due to the saints of the time, who renewed her spiritual life, and are still the great masters of ascetical and mystical living for our own day.

The Church's course could thus be followed stage by stage, at each of which trials and tribulations were overcome with the aid of those who in turn went before Christ's people, bearing the torch of holiness.

## ASPECTS OF CHRIST

If one wants to understand what saints do in the Church it must be remembered that one alone is holy, there is only one saint—Jesus Christ. Those we call saints are such purely through sharing in their Master's holiness. Enlivened by his spirit, they try to live as Jesus would have lived had he been in their place: their place in time, their place geographically, their place in human society.

The short earthly life of Jesus was lived in a particular country, during the reigns of the emperors Augustus and Tiberius, at the moment when the Jewish community into which he was born was on the point of breaking up. We know a few facts about his life from four short books, called gospels. For nineteen hundred years millions of men have reflected on every line of these books in their endeavour in their turn to live as he did; but they have never recovered the identical material and social conditions in which their Master passed his life. So they have had to transpose, for they could not simply copy: to have done so in a different context would have meant a lifeless, misleading picture. In order to be faithful to Christ's spirit, they had to strike out on their own, to innovate: more exactly, his spirit created something fresh in each one of them.

Furthermore, their temperaments, their characteristics, their whole nature, by birth and acquired, were not those of the Son of David. In them the spirit of Jesus worked on quite new material. So it is only to be expected that they should not look like a series of prints all taken from the same negative. Saints are astonishingly different from one another: and yet there is a family likeness about them, their common likeness to Jesus. Medieval stone-carvers rather suggested this when they represented the Twelve Apostles above the western doors of great churches, all drawn up in line on either side of their Master: in height, in build, in facial appearance they are all different. Yet there is something in common, a certain likeness to Jesus in each one.

There was a very great difference in state and character between St Antony and St Thomas More, between St Augustine and St Louis; and the difference was no less between the environment of each of them and Palestinian Jewry in the first century. They did not try to efface what was peculiar to them, but rather emphasized it; and it seems that by so doing they were enabled to develop certain traits of Jesus that he in his short ministry did not bring out fully. St Paul says that he made up in his own body whatever was lacking to the sufferings of Christ. May we not say with a like boldness that in their lives the saints made up whatever was lacking in Christ's earthly life?

Certain gospel references enable us to see the poverty that Jesus chose: it has been made more explicit and brought closer to our attention by St Francis. Jesus' concern for people's unhappy lot and his haste to help them was continued under a new and perhaps more far-reaching form by St Vincent de Paul.

Jesus' pity for repentant sinners lived again in St John Vianney's confessional, and his love for children flowered in the homes of St John Bosco.

Indeed, often the best way for the faithful to follow Jesus today is to take his saints for a pattern. They are nearer to us, more imaginable; the conditions in which they worked are often much more like ours. That does not mean that we need not constantly refer to the original divine pattern; but we should have overlooked some of Christ's characteristics had they not been emphasized by this one or that among those who lived according to his spirit far better than we do.

## PATRON SAINTS

It follows naturally from what has just been said that we as individuals are particularly attracted to one saint rather than to others, and that we put ourself under his or her protection, or "patronage", as his friends and followers did during his lifetime.

A predilection of that sort ought to govern the choice of patron saint that parents make when they give their child a name at baptism. Too often they choose a name simply because they like its sound, or because it is usual in the family, or because it is fashionable, without knowing anything about the saint who bore and sanctified the name. This is a pity. And it is not what the Church intends.

In early times, when baptism was to be given to an adult the candidate came forward with the name that had been given him at birth, and under that name he was baptized. It was devotion to the saints that suggested to parents that they should name their children after saints whom they particularly revered. Thus a custom grew up, which was general by the thirteenth century and is now a rule. Canon law directs that at baptism a name that is Christian be given: if the parents are not willing to do this, the minister has to add a saint's name to the one they have chosen, and to enter both names in the baptismal register.

As well as individuals, corporations of all kinds are invited to put themselves under the protection of a saint: "If all be done in order, it is praiseworthy that saints should be chosen by nations, dioceses, provinces, associations, religious families, and other places or moral persons [corporate bodies]; and that, if the Apostolic See confirms the choice, those saints should be their patrons" (Canon 1278). Thus St John Chrysostom has been named patron saint of preachers; St Teresa of Lisieux, with St Francis Xavier, of missions and missionaries throughout the world; St John Vianney of parish priests and others who have cure of souls; and many more.

## INTERCESSORS FOR US

It has been pointed out in Chapter IV that from early times Christians called confidently on the intercession of the martyrs in Heaven. St Jerome, St Ambrose, St Augustine and other fathers expounded the reasons for their trust, and they are the same as those advanced by later theologians. "The greater the charity of the saints, in their heavenly home, the more they intercede for those who are still on their journey and the more they can help them by their prayers; the more they are united with God, the more effective those prayers are. This is in accordance with divine order, which makes higher things react upon lower things, like the brightness of the sun filling the atmosphere" (St Thomas, *Summa Theologica*, II, II, Q. 83, art. 2).

They were, however, faced by a delicate question: How can the blessed know what happens on earth? In particular, how can they hear the prayers that are addressed to them?

Different answers are given, but all agree that the blessed cannot be indifferent to the objects for which they laboured when on earth or unmindful of those whom they loved. St Thomas says that each saint sees in the divine essence whatever is necessary to his bliss. Blessedness implies that all that is incomplete here below finds its fulfilment in God; and earthly affections being willed by God, they must at last come to full fruition in him. God cannot withhold from the blessed the ability to know, in his light, whatever is asked of them in prayer, or refuse them what they see good to ask him.

With some shades of variation, that is the teaching of all theologians. And it is interesting to find it perfectly expressed by a seventeenth-century Protestant, who was an acute philosopher, Leibniz: "The spirits of the blessed are now much closer to us than when they lived on earth . . ., their charity and desire to help us is much more eager, and their prayers now carry much more weight. On the other hand, we see all that God grants at the prayer of holy people who are still with us, and the consequent good of joining our brethren's prayers to our own. Therefore I cannot see why it should be looked on as wrong to invoke a soul in Heaven or one of the holy angels."

Leibniz only requires that "religious and prudent men should be careful to distinguish in all respects, including outward marks of honour, between the infinite worship due to God alone and the veneration (*dulia*) due to the saints". And in that all Catholics are in complete agreement with him.

CHAPTER IX

# THE HISTORY OF

# THE SAINTS

The influence of the saints in the Church has always been
strongest on those who lived close to them and so could benefit
immediately from their teaching and example. But their influence goes on after death through the accounts of them
written by those who knew them or knew of them. And as the
number of later readers is very much bigger than the number
of contemporaries, and goes on growing, it follows that the
written story of the saints keeps their influence alive and increases its effects indefinitely. It is important to notice that
many calls to holiness have been heard and answered through
reading the lives of saints.

## STORIES AND TALES

St Gregory the Great, who became pope in the year 590,
wrote four books of *Dialogues* about the saints of Italy, especially St Benedict. He tells us himself how he came to undertake
this work.

His office involved him in a burdensome amount of secular
duties, and he looked back with longing to the time when he
was a simple monk. He confided in his deacon, Peter: "My
distress is often aggravated", he told him, "by the thought of
this man or that who gave up the world wholeheartedly. I reflect
on the height that they have reached, and contrast it with the

low place where I still linger". Peter questioned his master
about these men of God, and expressed surprise that so little
should be heard about their miracles: "I do not doubt that we
have had holy people among us, but I do not think anyone has
seen them do miracles." It was in response to Peter's ignorance
that St Gregory wrote his *Dialogues*, which he proposed to call
"The Wonders of the Italian Fathers".

We know how Gregory set about this work from his letters
and from certain passages in the *Dialogues* themselves. For instance, he wrote to a bishop of Syracuse: "The brethren around
me vie with one another in urging me to write a short account
of what is known about the miracles wrought by the holy
fathers in Italy. For that purpose I am in great need of help
from your kindness: will you therefore inform me briefly about
the miracles that occur to your mind and about which you
happen to know. I remember that you told me something about
Master Nonnosus, the abbot, but I have forgotten what it was.
Please tell me about this, and about other things, if there are
any."

Gregory wrote similar letters to other bishops, whose names
he gives as references in the *Dialogues*. But there were others
besides bishops: "I cannot pass over in silence what I learned
hardly a fortnight ago", he writes. "An aged man, and poor,
was brought to me, and, as I like talking with old men, I asked
him with some interest where he came from. When he said it
was from Todi, I at once asked if he knew the bishop, Fortu-
natus. 'I knew him, and knew him well', he replied. So I said,
'Tell me, please, if you know any miracles of his, and help me
to learn what sort of man he was'. And he answered, 'He was
a very different man from those we see nowadays . . .' ".

The old man then told him what he had heard. St Gregory
did not feel called on to doubt what he was told, and wrote it
all down in good faith, to the great edification of his readers.

When he related St Benedict's miracles, Peter said, "These
are great things that you relate, very great things. They will

edify many people. The more of this very good man's miracles that I hear, the more I want to hear."

St Gregory was not a simpleton or a deceiver, any more than Sulpicius Severus or St Paulinus of Nola or St Gregory of Tours. He enables us to understand what was the mentality of hagiographers from the sixth century till the end of the Middle Ages. And the admiring exclamation of his deacon Peter shows the state of mind of their hearers and readers: "Miracles!—the more I hear, the more I want to hear!" When men wrote or listened to a saint's life, they were much less concerned to learn about what he had really done than to be enthralled by a good story. It appears that the verification of facts meant very much less to them than it does to us.

Already, a century before St Gregory, embroideries had begun to be added to the authentic accounts of martyrs, and whole pious fictions written when nothing could be found in the records. Some of these apocryphal works were otherwise excellent: the Passion of St Cecily, for example, is as lovely a praise of virginity as could be wished, and the office founded on it will move those who read it for a long time yet, even though they know that the story as it stands is imaginary.

For a thousand years few written lives of saints failed to conform to the rules of this literary *genre*, which required that everything about a saint should be idealized and decked in marvels. The masterpiece of this abundant literature is the collection made by a thirteenth-century Dominican, James of Voragine, who was archbishop of Genoa and is himself a *beatus*. It was written in Latin, and then translated into most European languages, with enormous success. It became known as the *Legenda Aurea*, which means in effect the Golden Book; but in English it is called the *Golden Legend*.[1]

[1] Caxton made the first edition printed in English, at Westminster in 1483. There have been modern English editions both of the *Golden Legend* and St Gregory's *Dialogues*. [Trans.]

## THE TRUTH ABOUT SAINTS

We are all of us susceptible to the attractions of a legendary tale well told, but in these days that is not what we look for in the story of a saint.

For us they are not mythical beings, something like the heroes of ancient Greece. Our reverence for them is not directed to a dolled-up image, but to the actual living person whom that image is supposed to represent. When we read the gospels we try to see Christ's human life in its fullness, in order that he may impart his divine life to us: in the same way, when we read saints' lives we want to know their difficulties, trials and conflicts, so that their courage and their victory may be a call and an incentive to follow their example. How could they open the way for us if from the start they were as different from us as their legends make out?—if they had lived from childhood in such a supra-mundane world as their biographers loved to present, a world in which babies refused the breast on Fridays out of a spirit of penance?

## THE UNKNOWN

If we want to tell the unadorned truth and make no statement that is not certain, we have to resign ourselves to the fact that there are many saints of whom little is known and many of whom nothing is known. This is the more difficult to stomach when we find that among them are some of the most famous. For instance, St George, protector of the kingdom of England (and of boy-scouts): all we know is that a martyred George was venerated in Syria from the fourth century, and that in the following century his tomb was shown at Lydda in Palestine. Of St Christopher, so long invoked by travellers and now particularly by motorists, nothing is known except that a church bearing his name was built at Chalcedon, near Constantinople, in 450. Nothing, again, is known about St Barbara, the patroness of miners and gunners.

The attractive legends that made these martyrs so popular took shape in the earlier Middle Ages, at a time when all authentic records of them had perished. Devotion to St George was popularized in England and France by crusading knights who had been encamped for a long time at Lydda. St Christopher's legend was doubtless suggested by the name given him at baptism, which means "Christ-bearer". As for St Barbara, particulars in her legend caused her to be depicted with a tower and to be invoked against sudden death, and so against lightning. Did the tower and the lightning suggest to those who handled explosives that they should put themselves under her protection? However that may be, we are a long way from reality and actual life.[1]

We may well take pleasure in legends, just as we like to read stories about King Arthur (which can, indeed, teach us something about the medieval spirit). But we ought to find yet more attraction in saints about whom we can know what they really were and did.

## THE WELL-KNOWN

There is no need for a saint to have written much for us to know what sort of man he was. We have only thirteen of St Paul's letters, some of them quite short, but they are enough to bring him very close to us, tingling with life, a man of most powerful character, sometimes harsh, sometimes overflowing with kindness, full of impassioned love for Christ Jesus.

We have many more writings of numerous other saints, and we can learn the secrets of their inner life from letters, sermons, private diaries. We cannot claim to know every detail of the life of St Augustine or St Bernard, of St Teresa of Avila or St Vincent de Paul: but we know much more about them than about the great men and women who are our contemporaries.

[1] The classical general work on all this subject is H. Delehaye's *Legends of the Saints* (London, 1907; revised French edition, Brussels, 1955).

Sometimes it is our good fortune to be able to come into contact with them by direct reading of their own works; there are excellent editions of those of St Teresa, St Francis de Sales, St Thomas More, St Vincent de Paul and many others.

But even more to the point there are the many good biographies of saints that have been published during the past fifty years, in English as well as in other languages, books written in a lively way and scrupulously careful of historical accuracy. With their help we can study these "new aspects of Christ" at leisure, and be drawn to follow them.

## THE UNCERTAIN

The historian's work is never easy. First he has to make a collection of all the documents that bear on his subject: these are *the sources*. Then he has to consider the value of his sources: are they authentic, and is their evidence well-informed and reliable? This is *criticism of sources*. He has then to use the sources that he has not rejected in such a way as to provide a clear account of what is known about the person or matter in hand.

For most of the earlier saints this task is very difficult, for surviving documents are often few and fragmentary. Often, too, they have been touched up, made over, or falsified. Reliable evidence of contemporaries has to be got at beyond and through these legends and interpolated texts. This involves years of patient research in libraries everywhere, and critical study of all the documents found: only then can a veracious history of a saint be written.

## THE BOLLANDISTS

There is a small group of learned men that has been engaged on this most important and gigantic task for over three hundred years. They are members of the Society of Jesus, and work in Belgium. They are called Bollandists, from Father John Bolland, who began their work, though he did not originate it.

The idea was conceived by Father Heribert Rosweyde, a man thirty years old, who was living at Antwerp at the beginning of the seventeenth century.

To meet the criticisms of Protestants and to cleanse the history of the saints from the fantasies by which it had been overlaid, Rosweyde resolved to go back to the sources. The idea was not to write the lives of saints afresh, but to publish the oldest texts available about each one of them in their integrity. It was a vast programme: for thirteen hundred saints he reckoned on bringing together manuscript lives which were in Belgian libraries, and the whole project was to comprise eighteen folio volumes. Rosweyde did much preparatory work, but when he died in 1629 nothing was ready for the printer. The continuation of the work was then entrusted to Father Bolland. His scheme was to publish the documents about all the saints anywhere, classifying them according to the dates of their annual feast-days. These documents were to be accompanied by critical commentaries and notes. After fourteen years' work the two volumes for January appeared: they were the first of the *Acta Sanctorum*, which now numbers sixty-seven folio volumes, with those for the saints of December yet to come.

John Bolland's collaborators were two men of outstanding historical ability, Father Godfrey Henskens (Henschenius) and Father Daniel Papebroch, who went from one European library to another in quest of manuscripts. During the second half of the seventeenth century the Bollandists achieved work that won the admiration of every scholar in Europe, and by the early years of the eighteenth the *acta* of saints had been published to the end of June. The work was then carried on by conscientious scholars but men of lesser genius, till towards the end of the century it was brought to a temporary halt by the suppression of the Society of Jesus and the French Revolution.

In 1837 the Bollandists were re-established, with their residence at Brussels, and again the work went ahead. The outstanding name during the mid-nineteenth century was that of

Father Victor De Buck. The end of October was reached in 1883, this month alone comprising thirteen volumes. A further period of intense activity followed, directed by Father Charles De Smedt and then by Father Hippolyte Delehaye, who was president of the Bollandist society from 1912 to 1941. He was succeeded by Father Paul Peeters and then by Father Maurice Coens.

The published *Acta Sanctorum* still only reach the middle of November, because the Bollandists' hagiographical activity now goes far beyond its main concern. Since 1882 they have published a periodical review, the *Analecta Bollandiana*, now in its seventy-fifth volume, which treats all matters relevant to the history of the saints with impeccable scientific probity. The labour of future scholars is lightened by a series of funda-mental works of profound erudition, grouped under the name of "Subsidia Hagiographica"; this series has reached its twenty-seventh number.

## LIVES OF THE SAINTS

The works of the Bollandists are not to be found in every library. In any case they are not intended for the public at large, but for historians and biographers, whose business it is to digest and diffuse the results of so much expert research. But a word of warning should perhaps be given here about a collection of saints' lives called *Les Petits Bollandistes*, which has often been reprinted since it first appeared a century ago. The title is misleading, for the Bollandists had nothing what-ever to do with the work, which as a whole is of very little value indeed.

During the past fifty years there have been some useful series of individual lives of saints published in several lan-guages. That called "Les Saints" now runs to over a hundred volumes, many of which are first-rate; a number of the lives in this series have been translated into English. As for popular collections of lives, one of the very best, in Father Delehaye's opinion, was the work of an eighteenth-century English priest. From its first publication in 1756–9, Alban Butler's *Lives of the Saints* was constantly reissued, more or less unaltered. Eventually it was thoroughly revised and supplemented by Father Herbert Thurston, S.J., and published in twelve volumes in 1926–38. This edition was further revised and republished in four volumes in 1956, the two-hundredth anniversary of the original publication. This work is of special utility because, while the text is adapted to the general reader, its bibliographies and notes provide material of value to students.

CHAPTER X

# THE HIDDEN SAINTS

After the First World War, people were impressed by the thought of the number of soldiers of all armies who had given their lives without their individual acts of heroism and selflessness ever becoming known; many of them lay in nameless graves. And so it came about that an Unknown Soldier was given honoured burial in a place of national resort, in Westminster Abbey in London, beneath the Arc de Triomphe in Paris, at the Arlington cemetery in the United States, and elsewhere.

There is a similar situation in respect of the millions of holy men and women, some of them perhaps greater in the eyes of God than canonized saints, who are unknown because they lived in obscurity or because their inward holiness was never recognized by their fellows. Their hiddenness serves to enhance their worth before God, but they are unknown to men and to the Church herself; they are not held up to the admiration of succeeding generations or put before us as models.

If a saint is to be known and to be recognized as a saint he must needs have a certain publicity—the word is used in no depreciatory sense.

## *LITERARY PUBLICITY*

There are few saints in recent times who have been more famous and turned to more trustingly by more people than St Teresa of Lisieux.

It is true that the particular spiritual flavour of her religion answers a need of our time. But just think what would have happened if the prioress of her convent, her own elder sister, had not had the happy thought of imposing on her the duty of writing down the memories of her childhood. We should not have had *The Story of a Soul*. For a few years Sister Teresa's memory would have been cherished in a small Norman convent, the memory of a deeply religious young nun, known for her charm and spirit of self-denial; her death at only twenty-four would have been deplored; and then she would have been forgotten.

But what in fact happened? Soon after her death her Carmelite sisters published her memoirs. The book had an astonishing success. Its very faults helped to make it popular; the mincingness of its style made its austere teaching acceptable, just as the pretty face of her touched-up portraits reconciled people to the severity of the nun's veil. World-wide war itself did not lessen enthusiasm: soldiers carried pictures of Sister Teresa in their pay-books, among the photographs of their family.

By 1907, ten years after her death, records of unusual graces granted at Sister Teresa's intercession were being printed in *The Story of a Soul*. In 1909 steps towards her beatification were initiated at Rome.[1]

All this happened in our time, when means of communication are endlessly multiplied by all the resources of printing. But even in the old days, when conditions were so much less favourable, many saints became known and were ultimately canonized because they happened to find a biographer. One of the most popular saints, not only of France but of Europe, was St Martin of Tours: in France, 500 villages and 4,000 parish-churches bear his name, and this popularity was, and is,

[1] The most recent English translation of the edited version of *The Story of a Soul* is by Michael Day, Cong. Orat. (London, 1951). A translation of the original version has been made by Mgr Ronald A. Knox entitled *The Autobiography of a Saint* (London and New York, 1958).

reflected in England. This is not only because St Martin's influence extended far beyond the Loire region during his lifetime; it is even more because a learned man of Aquitaine, Sulpicius Severus, met him several times at Tours and, after having been his guest at the monastery of Marmoutier, wrote his life. This biography was finished in 397, the year that Martin died, and Sulpicius Severus sent a copy of it to his friend St Paulinus of Nola. By the year 400 it was well known, and it was through the writings of Sulpicius Severus that St Martin became so famous.[1]

## FAMILY SPIRIT

There is one category of holy men and women whose holiness is brought to the Church's notice by even more powerful advocates than biographers, namely, by the religious families, orders or congregations, that they founded.

Francis of Assisi died on October 3rd, 1226; on July 29th, 1228, less than two years afterwards, he was canonized by Pope Gregory IX, who had previously been Cardinal Hugolino. As cardinal, he had been very closely associated with the development of the order of Friars Minor for ten years, presiding at its general chapters, directing its missions, helping Francis to draw up the successive texts of his rule. And while the pope was honouring the memory of Francis at Spoleto, Brother Elias was beginning to build the triple basilica on the hill at Assisi, where two years later the saint's tomb was sealed up in the crypt.

Not every founder of an order or congregation has been canonized so soon after his death; some have had to wait a hundred years or more. But when their foundations have flourished, their spiritual sons and daughters have shown their gratitude and filial devotion by pertinaciously forwarding the cause first of the beatification and then of the canonization of

[1] This Life of St Martin is translated by F. R. Hoare in *The Western Fathers* (London and New York, 1954).

their founders. The cause has not always reached a successful conclusion, but it has done so very often.

This can be seen at once by looking at the beatifications and canonizations of the past hundred years: religious founders and foundresses have the biggest place among them.

## THE CITY SET ON A HILL

"A city cannot be hidden if it is built on a mountain-top" (Matt. 5. 14). Jesus addressed those words to all his followers, but more directly to those in positions of leadership, spiritual and temporal, who have a special duty of being living examples. When they realize their responsibilities and live up to them in the way God looks for, men are not slow to notice their virtues. In people of lesser estate, virtues are apt to go unnoticed, and no one is likely to interest himself in the possible beatification of the persons concerned.

That is why there are among the canonized confessors very many more popes and bishops and abbots, even kings, than tradesmen and labourers and housewives. That does not mean that earthly hierarchies and classes are perpetuated in Heaven and that lesser folk are still in a subordinate position. The whole Gospel, and particularly the Beatitudes, teaches exactly the opposite: the kingdom of Heaven is for the poor and lowly. And indeed, when circumstances are such that public recognition by the Christian people draws the attention of the Church's authorities to one of these humble lives, and its holiness is made manifest, the honour that it receives is even more marked than usual. We think at once of Bernadette Soubirous or Mary Goretti.

All it comes to is that circumstances favourable to the necessary "publicity" are more often found when the people in question are leaders or in some substantial position than when they live lost among the crowd. The Church accords the distinction of public veneration to those whose holiness she has been able to verify; she does not claim to judge those whose cause has not been brought before her.

## THE FEAST OF ALL SAINTS

On All Saints' Day we celebrate all that multitude of holy men and women who are wholly unknown or known to but a few.

The churches of the East observed a yearly feast of the Martyrs of the Whole World in the fourth century. It was an appropriate and timely idea to think of all those who, during the persecutions of the preceding centuries, had died for Christ without their martyrdom coming to public knowledge. Those persecutions did not differ much from the persecutions of today. Think of all those Christians in the Near and the Far East who in recent years have given their lives rather than deny Jesus Christ and his Church.

In ancient Rome there was a famous circular temple, called the Pantheon because it was sacred to all the chief divinities of heathendom. In the year 609 or 610 Pope Boniface IV turned this temple into a Christian church, dedicating it in honour of the Blessed Virgin Mary and All the Martyrs. This was the origin of our feast of All Saints; it was not yet fixed for November 1st, but the principle was recognized; and little by little the idea of a commemoration, not only of all the martyrs but of all the confessors too, spread to the whole of the West. It is the feast of all those whom Christ has sanctified, of all those members of the holy people who have reached their heavenly home.

That place of blessedness is everybody's goal: of all those who are "of Christ", all whom he has sanctified, those who confess his name and the great multitude who, also called by him, do not yet know him. Numberless people are held up on the road because they have not yet been won over by saints, because the Christian *élite* is not yet holy enough. It is for this aristocracy of Christians to make ready tomorrow's harvest of saints.

# SELECT BIBLIOGRAPHY

LAVELLE, Louis: *The Meaning of Holiness* (translated from the French by Dorothea O'Sullivan, with an introduction by Dom Illtyd Trethowan), London, Burns & Oates, 1954; New York, Pantheon.

*Butler's Lives of the Saints* (edited, revised and supplemented by Herbert Thurston S.J. and Donald Attwater), four volumes, London, Burns & Oates, and New York, Kenedy, 1956. Each entry is followed by a useful bibliography.

*The Saints*. A Concise Biographical Dictionary (edited by John Coulson), London, Burns & Oates, and New York, Hawthorn, 1958.

DELEHAYE, Hippolyte, Bollandist: *The Legends of the Saints* (translated from the first French edition by V. M. Crawford), London and New York, Longmans, 1907.

THURSTON, Herbert, S.J.: *The Physical Phenomena of Mysticism*, London, Burns & Oates, Chicago, Regnery, 1952.

The following biographies of saints are suggested as a specimen list of some of the best works in this field:

ATTWATER, D.: *Martyrs: from St Stephen to John Tung*, Sheed and Ward, London and New York, 1957.

BRODRICK, James, S.J.: *Saint Francis Xavier*, London, Burns & Oates, New York, Farrar Strauss, 1952.

CHALLONER, Richard: *Memoirs of Missionary Priests*, first published London, 1741. The standard modern edition of this classic is that by J. H. Pollen, S.J., London, Burns & Oates, 1924.

CHAMBERS, R. W.: *Thomas More*, London, Cape, 1935, Newman, Westminster, Md, 1949.

CURTAYNE, Alice: *Saint Catherine of Siena*, London, Sheed and Ward, 1929.

CUTHBERT of Brighton, Fr, O.F.M. Cap.: *Saint Francis of Assisi*, London, Longmans, 1912; new edition, New York, 1948.

DANIEL-ROPS, Henri: *Les Aventuriers de Dieu,* Paris, Artheme Fayard, 1951. (Now in translation for American publication.)
————: *St. Paul, Apostle of Nations,* Chicago, Fides, n.d.

DAWES, Elizabeth, and BAYNES, Norman H.: *Three Byzantine Saints,* Oxford, Blackwell, 1948.

DUDDEN, F. H.: *Life and Times of Saint Ambrose,* two volumes, Oxford, University Press, 1935.

SHEPPARD, L. C., tr.: *St Vincent de Paul* by Mgr J. Calvet, New York, McKay, 1952.

THORNTON, Francis Beauchesne: *The Burning Flame, The Life of Pius X,* New York, Benziger, 1952.

WAUGH, Evelyn: *Edmund Campion,* London, Hollis & Carter, 1947. Boston, Little, Brown.

# The Twentieth Century Encyclopedia of Catholicism

*The number of each volume indicates its place in the over-all series and not the order of publication.*

*All titles are subject to change.*

## DATE DUE

| | | | |
|---|---|---|---|
| | | | |
| | | | |
| | | | |
| | | | |
| | | | |
| | | | |
| | | | |
| | | | |
| | | | |
| | | | |
| | | | |
| | | | |
| | | | |
| | | | |
| | | | |
| | | | |
| | | | |